GardeningWithChildren

By Monika Hannemann, Patricia Hulse, Brian Johnson,
Barbara Kurland, and Tracey Patterson

SAm Tomasello
Illustrator

Sigrun Wolff Saphire
Editor

Parents and caregivers, please see pages 109 to 115 for an introduction to gardening with children and tips for using this book.

Sigrun Wolff Saphire
Senior Editor

Janet Marinelli
Consulting Editor

Elizabeth Peters
Consulting Editor

Joni Blackburn
Copy Editor

Mark Tebbitt
Science Editor

Julia Reich Design | juliareichdesign.com
Art Direction

Steven Clemants
Vice-President, Science & Publications

Scot Medbury
President

Elizabeth Scholtz
Director Emeritus

Judith D. Zuk
President Emeritus

Handbook #187

Copyright © 2007 by Brooklyn Botanic Garden, Inc.

All-Region Guides, formerly 21st-Century Gardening Series,
are published three times a year at 1000 Washington Ave., Brooklyn, NY 11225.

Subscription included in Brooklyn Botanic Garden subscriber
membership dues ($35 per year; $45 outside the United States).

ISBN 13: 978-1-889538-30-3
ISBN 10: 1-889538-30-2

Printed by OGP in China.
Printed on recycled paper.

GardeningWithChildren

contents

CHAPTER 1

Living in a Community

Take a look outside your window, and you are sure to see some wonders of the natural world: a bee buzzing by the flowers in your window box, the oak tree planted along the sidewalk swaying in the wind, or a squirrel gathering acorns.

All these creatures are part of nature's community, and their lives are connected in many ways. That squirrel outside your window depends on the oak tree for food and shelter. The oak tree in turn depends on the squirrel to gather its acorns and bury them in the ground—so that some of them will become the next generation of oak trees. These kinds of relationships are everywhere in nature. If you take away just one part (say, the oak tree), the entire community feels the loss.

Human beings depend on communities too. We need farmers to grow our food, bus drivers to take us to work or school, and doctors to take care of us when we are sick.

Right in your very neighborhood you depend on your community. You can call on your next-door neighbors to water your plants when you go on vacation. You can go outside and play with other kids down the block.

What may surprise you is that a healthy garden is also an interdependent community of plants and animals, including people. Let's take a closer look and find out how gardens and natural communities work!

Nature Neighborhood

In your neighborhood, you probably know where your best friend lives and where your school is. But do you know who lives in your nature neighborhood? You can find nature neighborhoods in your backyard, a local park, or even a flower box sitting outside your kitchen window. Let's find out more.

Nature Journal

A nature journal is a fun way to
record what you find in your nature
neighborhood—and many other
things you will discover in this book.
To get started, you'll need a blank diary or
a notebook.

Sit somewhere so that you can see as much of
your nature neighborhood as possible. Use
crayons or colored pencils to draw everything you
see in your journal.

If you like, include sounds. If you hear a bird chirping from
the top of a tree, write "chirp" at the top of the tree in your
drawing. Are there any sounds you don't recognize?

Pick a day in each season of the year to draw what you see. From
season to season, do you always see the same plants and animals?

The Living Soil

In the natural world, there is so much more than meets the eye! Entire communities of insects, plants, and animals live hidden away from view. Take soil, for example. Right underneath the surface, you'll find countless critters making their homes. Underground is another one of the interdependent communities found in nature. Hard to believe? Let's explore the living soil.

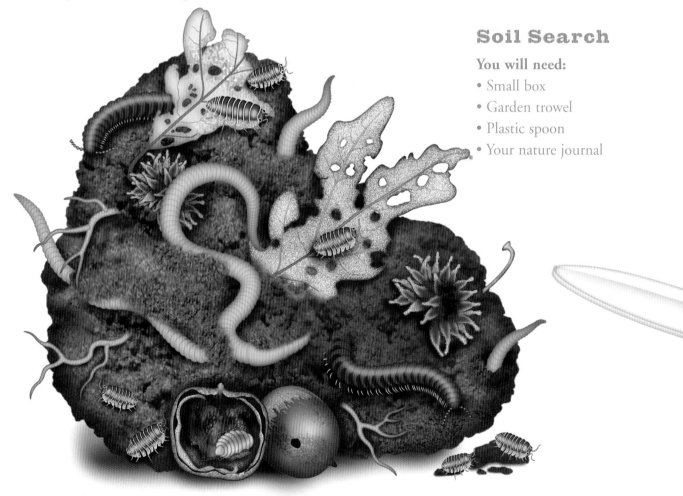

Soil Search

You will need:
- Small box
- Garden trowel
- Plastic spoon
- Your nature journal

Earthworms help keep the soil healthy! Their tunnels allow air into the soil. Their castings (poop) provide important soil nutrients such as nitrogen. There may be anywhere from 50,000 to 1½ million earthworms in one acre of healthy soil.

What to do:

1. Find a place in your nature neighborhood where it is okay to dig in the ground. (If your nature neighborhood is in your local park, be sure to ask a park ranger if you may dig up a small sample of soil.) Use your garden trowel to dig up a few scoops of soil, and place the soil in the box.

2. Using the plastic spoon and your fingers, explore your soil sample. If you find insects or earthworms, handle them gently so that you don't hurt them.

3. Who lives in your soil? Draw in your nature journal one of the living creatures you find.

4. What else do you find in your soil sample? Write down the names of all the things you find there. If you don't know the name of something, either give it a name of your own or just describe what it looks like. How many different things did you find in your soil?

5. When you are finished exploring, return the soil to the same spot where you dug it up.

6. Now, dig up a small sample of soil from your garden, and place that soil in your empty box.

7. Use the plastic spoon and your fingers again to explore the soil. How is this soil different from the soil in your nature neighborhood?

Soil Critters

sweetgum fruit

earthworm

millipede

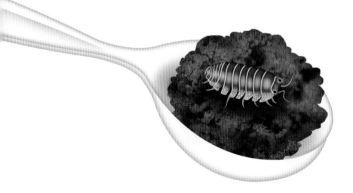

Root Views

As you explored the living soil in the previous activity, you likely found insects, earthworms, twigs, and stones. What you may not realize, however, is that plants are growing, moving, and changing below the surface of the earth as well. Think about carrots: The yummy orange part that we (and rabbits in our gardens) like to eat actually grows belowground. How can we get to see this exciting growth happening?

Root-View Garden

A "root-view garden" allows you to watch plants growing in the soil. It's easy to make and even more fun to observe. Here's how you can do it right in your kitchen at home!

You will need:
- Half-gallon milk carton (a coated cardboard box, not a plastic jug)
- Clear plastic wrap
- Strong tape, like packing tape or duct tape
- Scissors
- Potting soil
- Carrot seeds
- Radish seeds

The roots of plants help hold soil together and prevent erosion.

What to do:

Use your scissors to cut off the top of the milk carton.

Poke a hole in the side of the milk carton and cut out a square, about 4 inches high and 4 inches wide. (If you'd like a second viewing window, cut another hole the same size on the opposite side of the carton.)

Cut a piece of plastic wrap to fit over each window. Tape it on all sides to hold it tightly in place. Now comes the fun part!

Fill the carton with soil and plant a few of the carrot and radish seeds. Water the soil and put the carton in a sunny place.

Over the next few weeks, keep your "root-view" garden watered and watch the action through your viewing windows!

Garden Community

So far in this chapter, we have explored some of the nature communities around us. Now, let's explore our gardens. Whether your garden is in your backyard or on your windowsill, remember that a garden is a community of interdependent plants, insects, and other animals—including us! Before we investigate how all of these things interact with each other, let's learn a little bit more about the various members of our garden community.

Garden Herbarium

A herbarium is a collection of dried and pressed plants. Many botanic gardens have a herbarium as a kind of encyclopedia of their plant species, as well as species from around the world. You can make a herbarium for your garden as a way of getting to know all the plants that are growing there. Making your garden herbarium will take a while: You will only be able to collect, press, and dry a few plants at a time. However, over the course of a full growing season, from early spring to late fall, you can probably make a record of all of the plants in your garden. If you don't know the name of a plant, use a field guide or garden book to identify it. (If you don't have one, look on page 115 for suggestions.)

You will need:
- Newspaper
- Cardboard (cereal boxes will do)
- Several heavy books
- Scissors or garden pruning shears
- Your nature journal
- Glue

One of the largest herbaria in the world is at the Royal Botanic Gardens, Kew, in London, England. This herbarium has collected and preserved more than 7 million plant specimens!

What to do:

1. Carefully cut a small piece (about 4 to 6 inches long) from several plants in your garden, including a leaf or several leaves. Don't take a cutting from a young or very small plant.

2. Take the plant cutting inside. On your work table, place a piece of cardboard. Lay two pieces of newspaper on top of it.

3. Lay your plant cutting on the newspaper. Cover it with two more newspaper sheets and another piece of cardboard.

4. Record the name of the plant, along with the date and the location from which you collected it.

5. Lay down two more sheets of newspaper and repeat this process until all of your plants have been placed in a stack.

6. Carefully set the stack in a cool, dry spot and place several heavy books on top of it. Press the plants for several days, until they dry completely.

7. Gently remove the dry plants from your press and glue them into your journal.

Basil
Date: August 7
Where found: my garden

Garden Explorations

You may be surprised by the changes that happen in your garden all the time. Plants grow. Different animals stop by for a visit or move in for good. How is everyone working together day and night?

Nighttime Safari

Plan a nighttime safari to explore your garden. You might want to choose an evening with a full moon to help you see better.

Make a list in your nature journal of the things you find. What differences do you notice between your nighttime and daytime observations?

Garden Puppet Show

The members of your garden community are like the characters in a play. There are stars and characters with smaller parts. There's a crew to build the set and a director to put the show together. Each has an important role to play. Write the story of your garden and perform it for your family and friends!

You will need:
- Colored pencils, crayons or markers, and strong paper
- Craft sticks and glue
- Leaves, petals, seeds, and other plant parts
- Other supplies like yarn, glitter, pipe cleaners, cotton balls, and ribbon

What to do:

1 Make a list of the plants, insects, and other garden community members you want to include in your puppet show.

2 Write the script for your puppet show, giving each character a role. Try to tell the story of your garden community, including how the plants and insects in your garden depend on one another. Who will be the star?

3 Make stick puppets for your characters. You can use real leaves or flower petals to make your characters more true to life.

Garden Companions

Think for a minute about your best friends. You probably love hanging out with them, playing games and having fun. You might also help each other with homework and talk to each other when you have a problem. The most important thing is that you support each other and help each other to learn and grow. Plants in your garden rely on each other for support too. People have recognized the combinations of plants that help each other grow well for hundreds, if not thousands, of years. Here are a few examples you can try.

Three Sisters Garden

One of the oldest known examples of companion planting is the native American three sisters garden. The Iroquois people in northeastern North America found great success in planting the trio of corn, beans, and squash. How do they work together?

Corn provides a pole for the bean plants to climb. Beans add precious nitrogen (fertilizer) to the soil. Low-growing squash covers the soil, helping to keep in moisture and shading out weeds.

The three sisters also provide us with a good balance of nutrition. Corn is a good source of carbohydrates, beans give us protein, and squash is full of important vitamins.

You will need:
- Corn, bean, and squash seeds
- Garden hoe
- Garden trowel

What to do:

In late spring or early summer, loosen the ground in your garden with your hoe.

Form some soil into a small mound, about 1 foot high and about 2 feet across. (If you are going to plant several mounds, make sure they are at least 3 feet apart.)

Plant six corn seeds in a wide circle in the top of the mound.

Water your garden and watch your corn plants grow. When they are 6 inches tall, plant a circle of six bean seeds around your corn plants, about 6 inches out.

One week after the beans, plant five squash seeds in a circle, about 1 foot out from the bean plants.

Observe the plants as they begin to grow. Weed out the weaker plants, leaving just one or two of the strongest of each of the three sisters. In time, the beans will spiral around the cornstalks and the squash will cover the ground below!

We Grow Together

Basil helps improve the flavor of tomatoes, and it keeps away flies and mosquitoes.

basil   tomato

Chives boost the growth and flavor of carrots.

carrot   chives

Pesky cucumber beetles keep their distance from oregano!

cucumber   oregano

Bullies in the Garden

Weeds are the plants that every gardener loves to hate! It's not that these plants are bad in and of themselves. It's just that sometimes weeds can make it more difficult to grow the plants we want to grow in our gardens. Certain plants can be so aggressive that they outcompete and even kill other plants in a fight for survival. If you don't pull the weeds in your garden, they might take over and keep the plants that you planted from growing as well as they could.

Weed Patch

Set aside one small part of your garden (maybe a 2-foot square) to let weeds grow wild! (You can also use a pot if you'd rather not do this in your garden.) Plant some vegetable or flower seeds in the area that you set aside. Don't pull any plants that appear. What happens to the seeds that you planted? What would your garden look like if you didn't pull out the weeds on a regular basis?

A weed is a plant growing where you don't want it.

Growing Space

One of the ways that weeds take over is by crowding out your garden plants. Many garden plants are very particular about how and where they grow. They need just the right amount of sun, the perfect amount of water, and generally some "elbow" room between each other. Many weeds, however, can grow in just about any conditions—hot or cold, wet or dry, crowded or plenty of room. Let's see how one common garden flower, the marigold, responds to cramped quarters.

You will need:
- 1 package of marigold seeds
- 3 flowerpots
- Potting soil
- Watering can

What to do:
Fill your three pots with potting soil. Use a pencil or your finger to make small holes in the soil, about 1/4 inch deep.

In the first pot, make the holes about 1/4 inch apart. In the second pot, make the holes about 1 inch apart. In the third pot, make the holes about 2 inches apart.

Place a marigold seed in each hole and cover the seeds with a thin layer of soil. Place the pots in a sunny spot, and water them often enough to keep the soil damp.

Observe the plants as they begin to grow. What differences can you see? Which plants are taller or look healthier? Do they prefer growing close together or with lots of space?

Friend or Foe?

Just like aggressive plants, some animals and insects can do more harm than good in our gardens. Rabbits might nibble on some vegetables before we harvest them, and slugs can kill some plants by munching on their leaves. Of course, not all animals and insects are out to get your garden! In fact, beneficial insects help your garden in a number of ways, from controlling populations of insects that can harm your garden plants to pollinating plants when they flower.
Let's take a look at some of the critters in our gardens.

Who Is Your Friend?

Ladybugs eat aphids and mites, which can destroy plants in your garden. The verdict: Friend!

Aphids suck sap from plants. (Luckily, they are a favorite food of ladybugs and other beneficial insects.)
The verdict: Foe!

Slugs eat decaying plants, but they also help themselves to the living plants growing in your garden. The verdict: Foe!

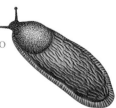

Spiders eat lots of insects that left unchecked might devour your plants.
The verdict: Friend!

Rabbits love most of the foods in your garden! Keep them out with a simple fence, buried several inches down into the soil.
The verdict: Foe!

Bumblebees buzz from plant to plant. Just what are those big fuzzy things doing? They're pollinating plants!
The verdict: Friend!

How do you keep critters from eating your garden? A few farmers' tactics worth trying: aluminum pie pans twirling on string, plastic owls perched on a fencepost and moved often, bars of soap or small net bags of hair dangling from a branch.

Scarecrow

Hungry birds have always given farmers and gardeners problems. To try to keep pesky birds away, scarecrows were placed in fields and orchards. By dressing scarecrows to look like real people, farmers hoped the "person" in the field would frighten off birds! It didn't always work—many birds soon learned that the scarecrow was just sitting there and would not chase them away. Today, most people use scarecrows just for decoration.

You will need:

- Old long-sleeved shirt
- Old pair of pants
- Old pair of socks or shoes
- Garden gloves
- Hat
- Safety pins
- String
- Old pillowcase
- Straw or newspaper for stuffing
- Markers or paint

What to do:

1. Tie shut the cuffs of the shirt and pants, and stuff the clothes with straw or newspaper. Stuff the socks and gloves and tie off the ends of these, too.

2. Using the safety pins, attach the gloves to the bottom of the shirtsleeves and the socks to the bottom of the pant legs. Tuck the shirt into the pants and pin them together.

3. Make the scarecrow's head. Draw or paint a face on the pillowcase, stuff it, and attach it with safety pins to the top of the shirt.

4. Top off your scarecrow with a hat, and don't forget to pin the hat on so it doesn't blow away!

5. Prop your scarecrow up against a fence, or attach it to a pole somewhere in your garden.

Your Place in the Garden Community

At this point, you are a nature communities expert! You have learned about many of the different communities in the natural world as well as in gardens. You have also seen how the plants and insects in a garden depend on each other for health and survival. Last but not least, you have learned about plants' need for sunlight, water, and space.

Dream Garden Design

You also have an important role in the garden community. After all, you decide what to plant and where to plant it. The rest of the garden community also needs you to pull weeds, add water to the soil, and monitor for insects and pests. Without this extra care, your garden would be a gigantic mess!

Keeping in mind everything you've learned about garden communities, what would your ideal garden look like? This is your chance to think ahead to next year's garden and make a plan for it. You might want to do this activity in the winter when you'll be spending plenty of time indoors. You'll also want to return to this activity as you continue to read and do activities from the rest of this book.

GARDEN PLAN

In your nature journal, draw a plan for your perfect garden community. Before you begin, you may want to make a list of all the plants, insects and other animals, and other garden elements that are important for you to include. Make your drawing as real as possible so you can use it as a guide for planting. What have you decided to include? Why?

Did you know? There are more than 70 million gardeners in the United States and Canada.

My Garden Plan

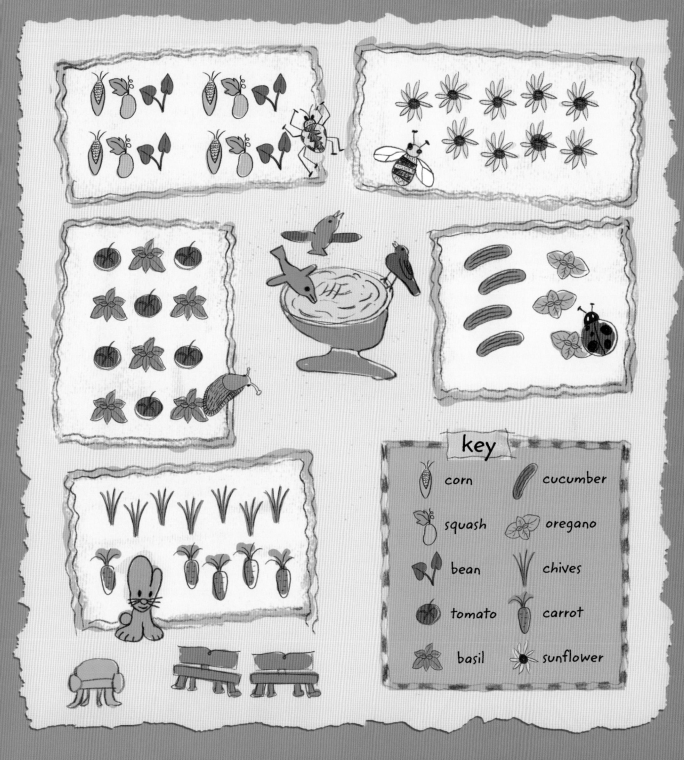

key

corn   cucumber

squash   oregano

bean   chives

tomato   carrot

basil   sunflower

CHAPTER 2

Plants Are Essential for Life

If you had to choose a single favorite food to eat for breakfast, lunch, or dinner, what would it be? Does thinking about food make you feel hungry? Do plants ever get hungry the way people do? Wait a minute—that's a silly question! Plants don't move from place to place the way people do, so they cannot simply jump up and get a bite to eat. Yet plants, like people and other animals and all living things, need a source of energy—or fuel—to keep their body systems working and a source of materials to build their bodies. They need fuel to make roots, stems, leaves, flowers, fruits, and seeds, but they cannot move in search of it, so how do they get it? They make their own. Sounds

seed

simple enough ... but how? Plants combine two ingredients that they collect from their environment, water and carbon dioxide gas, to produce sugar, a high-energy product that can also be used to help make the complex building materials they require for growth. The scientific word "photosynthesis" holds the key to the powerful source of energy that plants use to make sugar: Photo means "light" and synthesis means "to make." Light energy from the sun, shining down on the earth each day, powers the sugar-making process that keeps plants alive and provides energy for most living things on our planet!

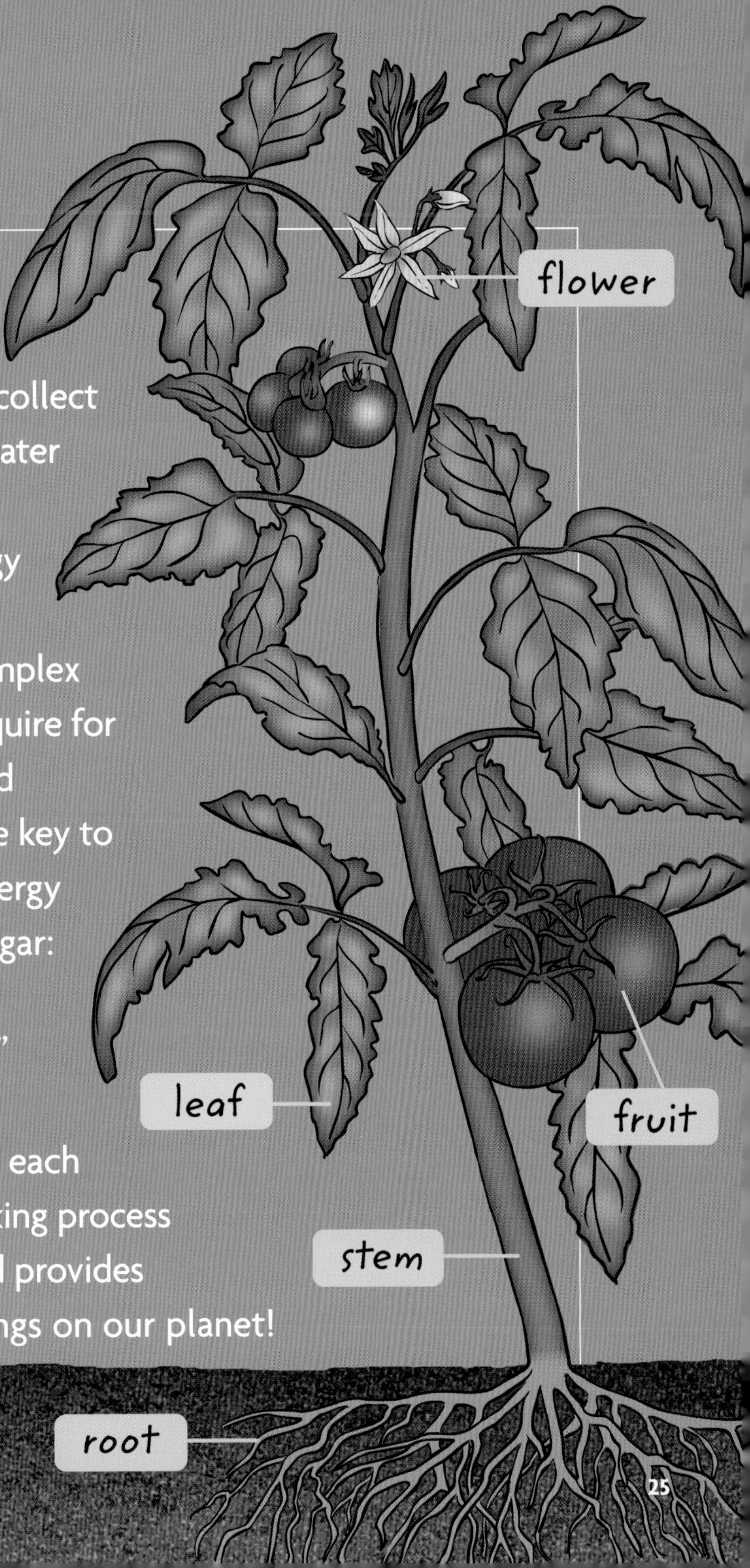

flower

leaf

fruit

stem

root

25

Plant Parts
Grocery Store Botany

Plants grow and live their lives in one place. They collect air, water, minerals, and sunlight, and make their own fuel. Each part of a plant's body has a job that helps the plant live and make seeds so that a new generation of plants can begin.

Plant Parts Shopping List

Plants grow roots, stems, leaves, flowers, fruits, and seeds. You can find all these plant parts in your garden. What may surprise you is that you can also find them at the grocery store.

What roots will you find at the store?

Did you know that when you eat broccoli you are eating flower buds?

Fruits are the parts of plants that have seeds. Do all fruits taste sweet?

What other plant parts can you find at the store?

Make a shopping list!

SHOPPING LIST

ROOT
Carrot
Radish

LEAF
Spinach
Lettuce

STEM
Celery*
Asparagus

FLOWER
Broccoli
Cauliflower

SEED
Sunflower
Sesame

FRUIT
Tomato
Cucumber

*Actually, botanists call it a leaf stalk.

Do you know why potatoes make good detectives? Because they keep their eyes peeled!

Made-Up Plant

Let's put a plant together with our plant parts from the grocery store.

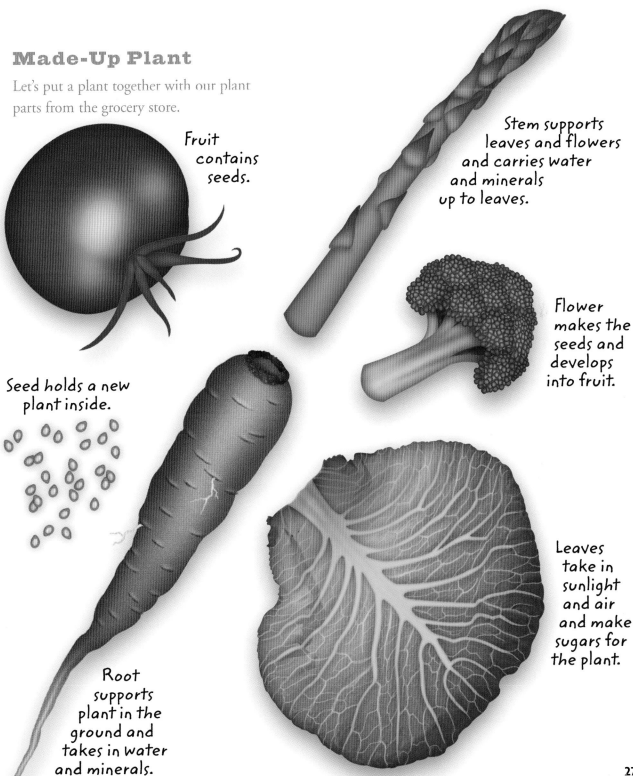

Fruit contains seeds.

Stem supports leaves and flowers and carries water and minerals up to leaves.

Flower makes the seeds and develops into fruit.

Seed holds a new plant inside.

Leaves take in sunlight and air and make sugars for the plant.

Root supports plant in the ground and takes in water and minerals.

Plant Parts Salad

Do you eat plants? Maybe you grow some vegetables in your garden. Plants make their own fuel and store it in their roots, stems, and leaves. Many plants also make delicious fruits. When we eat fruits, we can help the plant by saving the seeds and dispersing them. Seeds have energy stored inside to nourish the new plants they contain. Which plant parts do you like to eat?

What COLORS are in your salad?

Which plant parts are JUICY or CRUNCHY or SOFT or CRISP?

Do any taste SWEET or SPICY or TANGY or SAVORY?

Recipe for Salad

You will need:
- Large bowl
- 12 lettuce and/or spinach leaves
- 4 radish roots
- 2 carrot roots
- 2 tomato fruits
- 2 cucumber fruits
- 4 celery and/or asparagus stems
- Cauliflower, broccoli, or nasturtium flowers
- Toasted sesame, sunflower, or peanut seeds

What to do:

1 Wash the lettuce or spinach leaves, drain the water away, and cut or tear them into bite-sized pieces. Put them in the bowl.

2 Wash the radish and carrot roots and cut them into circles. What color are they on the outside? What color are they on the inside?

3 Wash and cut the celery and/or asparagus stems into bite-sized pieces. Can you see the tubes in the celery stem? They carry water.

4 Wash the tomato and cucumber fruits. Slice them into circles or wedges. Look for the seeds.

5 Arrange all your vegetables in a large bowl. Sprinkle some sesame, sunflower, or peanut seeds on your salad, and enjoy!

ROOT-TOP GARDEN

Radish, carrot, turnip, and beet tops can grow into plants all over again!
- You'll need an aluminum pie pan or takeout container from a restaurant. Punch a few holes in the bottom of the pan with a pencil point so water will drain out. Place the pan on a tray.
- Add a layer of soil about 2 inches deep.
- Place root tops in the soil with their cut bottoms down. Trim the tops of any leaves that are still attached, but leave about an inch of the leaf stems.
- Place your garden in a sunny window and keep the soil evenly moist.
- Observe your root-top garden every day and watch for leaves to start to grow and for small roots to grow out of the root tops into the soil.

A farmer does not plant carrots, beets, turnips, and radishes by cutting up the vegetables and replanting the tops! Farmers plant seeds and grow them, and then they harvest them!

29

Photosynthesis— To Make With Light

We all know that plants need sunlight to live. What do they do with sunlight? Light is a form of energy. Living things need energy to keep their bodies active and to develop and grow. Animals, like people, get their energy from the foods they eat. Plants get their energy differently. They follow a recipe, combining two major ingredients, water and carbon dioxide, to produce an energy-rich product—sugar!

Green Power

People and animals can get sunlight, carbon dioxide, and water, yet they are not able to use those things to make sugar. What gives plants this special ability? The answer is in their color. Plants contain chlorophyll, a green pigment that traps sunlight energy. Plants use the sunlight energy to put water and carbon dioxide together to make sugar. Every green part of a plant has chlorophyll. Every green part of a plant makes sugar.

Plants make another product during photosynthesis that almost all living things on earth require to live: oxygen. Most of the oxygen in the earth's atmosphere is made by green plants that grow on land and green algae that live in the oceans. When the sun rises, chlorophyll goes to work trapping light and using it to make sugar and release oxygen.

Plants make oxygen, but they use it, too, just like people and other animals. When they break down sugars, plants need oxygen to release the energy needed to keep their bodies going and growing.

Chlorophyll Prints

You can extract the chlorophyll from a plant part and create a beautiful image when you make a chlorophyll print.

You will need:

- Green leaves collected from vegetables like spinach or kale
- Green leaves collected from herbs like basil or mint
- Green leaves collected from trees or shrubs (Get permission before removing leaves from a living plant.)
- Fabric—Use pieces of an old bedsheet or other flat, smooth fabric cut into squares, OR
- Paper—watercolor paper is best, since it is thicker and will absorb pigment
- Metal or wooden spoon
- Masking tape
- Strong flat surface like a table

What to do:

1. Fold your piece of fabric or paper in half and then open it up again.

2. Place a leaf, top side facing down, on one half of the fabric or paper surface and refold the fabric or paper back over the leaf. Tape the folded paper or fabric to the table to hold it in place.

3. Using the bottom of the spoon and pressing very firmly, rub the spoon across the fabric or paper. Hold the fabric or paper down firmly with your other hand.

4. Be sure to rub the spoon over the entire leaf area so that all the leaf's chlorophyll will be transferred onto the fabric or paper.

5. You can laminate or frame your chlorophyll prints. Or collect them in your nature journal. Do different leaves "print" different shades of green?

Solar Collectors Up Close

What parts of plants are green? These are the parts that contain chlorophyll, the green pigment that traps sunlight energy, which is used by plants to make food. On most plants, leaves are the major "food factories." Their job is to collect as much light as possible.

Looking at Leaves

Try to find four or five different leaves on plants in your garden, on trees, on plants growing indoors in your home, or on plants in your refrigerator.

What do your leaves have in common? How are they different from each other?

Turn your leaves over and observe the pattern of the veins. Botanists (scientists who study plants) call this pattern the venation of the leaf. The narrow tubes that form the network of venation throughout the blade of the leaf carry water, dissolved minerals, and sugars.

Use your finger to trace the pattern of the venation in each of your leaves.

Sketch the leaves and their vein patterns into your journal.

Botanists can identify a plant by studying its leaves. They use specific characteristics of a leaf, including its size, shape, color, surface texture, vein pattern, and edge pattern. They take note if the leaf is waxy, hairy, or fragrant when it is rubbed.

Some leaves are very narrow and thin, like pine needles. Can they still create a "solar collection surface"? Of course! Plants that make these types of leaves are trying to save water. They usually keep the needles on their branches all the time—they stay evergreen—even in winter when the air is very dry.

Leaves Up Close

Name of plant: spinach

Name of plant: honey locust

Ginkgo

Color: _____

Shape: _____

Length: _____

Width: _____

Texture: _____

Scent: _____

Where leaf was found: _____

Oak

Maple

Water, Water, Everywhere— Or Is There?

What do the plants in your house need to live and grow? How do you take care of them? You place them in a sunny window to get light. You make sure they have a roomy pot with soil so their roots have a place to grow. And you water them! Where would the water come from if you didn't turn on your faucet, fill your watering can, and give your plants a drink? Indoors, plants need people to give them water. Who waters the plants outside? Rain! The plants get as much water as the amount of rain that falls. What happens if there is little or no rain? What will happen to the plants that depend on water?

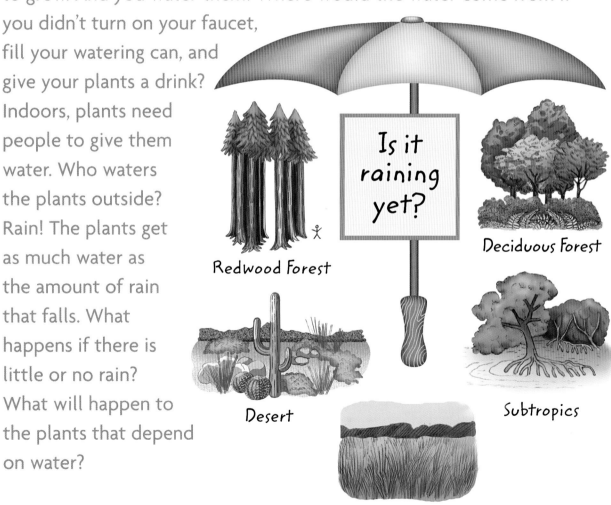

Is it raining yet?

Redwood Forest

Deciduous Forest

Desert

Subtropics

Prairie

Do you think a cactus from the desert would grow very well in a tropical rain forest? Would a tropical vine grow well in a desert? Plants from different environments are adapted to survive the challenges of the places they are originally from.

How Much Water Is Enough?

Plants that live in deserts get very little water. Plants that live in rain forests get lots! Plants that live in these different habitats have strategies for survival. What happens to your plants when they get too little water—less than they are used to getting? How do they appear? Can plants get too much water? Let's do an experiment to find out!

You will need:
- 6 bean seeds
- 3 pots
- Potting soil
- Watering can
- Sunny window
- Tray to go under each pot

What to do:

1. Fill pots with soil. Plant two seeds in each pot about 1/2 inch deep. Use any kind of bean, but use the same kind for all three pots.

2. When the plants are about 3 inches tall, number the pots 1, 2, and 3. If two bean plants start growing in your pot, pinch out the weaker-looking plant.

3. Water plant #1 twice a week.

4. Water plant #2 every day, even if the soil is wet.

5. Water plant #3 once every two weeks.

6. Set up a chart in your journal to record your observations. Do some research about bean plants. Where in the world did beans originate? How much rain falls in that area? Knowing that will give you an idea of the amount of water bean plants usually get.

7. Write down or draw your observations of the three plants. How does a gardener know how much to water a plant?

How Much Light Can a Leaf Collect?

Leaves come in many shapes and sizes. Some plants have big broad leaves, while others have very small narrow leaves. Some leaves have curvy edges, and others have many points. Plants arrange their leaves along and around their stems so that each of them can catch as much sunlight as possible. On most plants, the leaves are the major solar energy collectors! Does the shape of a leaf have anything to do with how much light it can collect? How can we measure the amount of surface a leaf presents to the sun?

Food for thought: Some plants, including cacti, have leaves that are so thin and narrow they are reduced to being spines! Without broad leaves, what part of the cactus collects sunlight for photosynthesis?

Measuring the Surface Area of a Leaf

You will need:
- Piece of graph paper with 1/2-inch squares
- Leaf
- Sharp pencil

What to do:

1 Place the leaf on the graph paper and trace the edge of the leaf as accurately as possible, keeping your pencil point close to the leaf edge.

2 Remove the leaf from the paper.

3 Count the number of boxes inside the leaf tracing. If a line does not fill a box completely, estimate how much of the box is included.

4 Repeat the process with one or more leaves of different size or shape. Compare the number of totals from all the leaves that you have traced.

DOT-DOT-DOT

You can also use dot stickers to compare leaf surface areas. Tape a leaf down to a piece of paper and place sticky dots on top of the leaf until the entire surface is covered. Count the number of dots. Repeat the process with different leaves. Compare the number of dots that cover up the surface of different leaves.

Design of a Food Factory

Photosynthesis takes place in the dark green areas called chloroplasts. (These contain chlorophyll.)

Cuticle
a waxy, waterproof coating

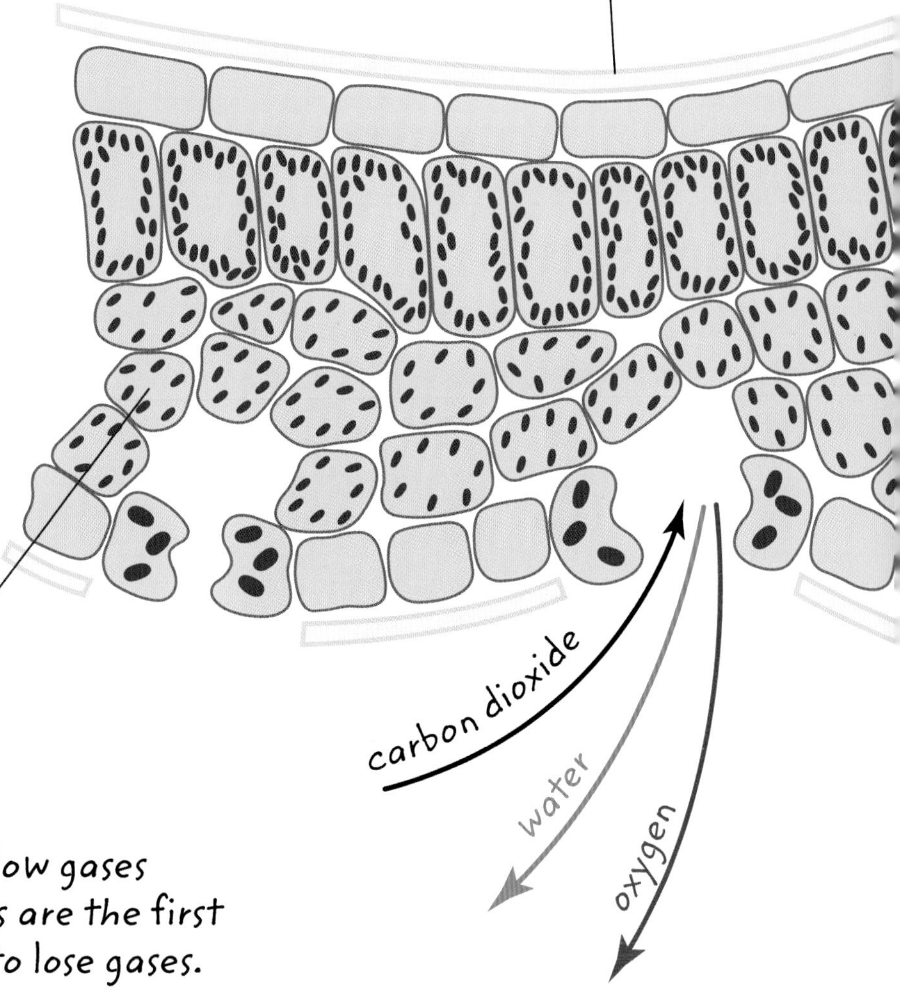

carbon dioxide

water

oxygen

Spongy Layer
Loosely packed cells allow gases to circulate; these cells are the first to absorb and the last to lose gases.

When plants breathe through their leaves, opening their pores called stomata, water escapes, evaporating into the air. If too much water is lost, the plant can wilt! The stomata can be closed on very hot or very windy days to conserve water.

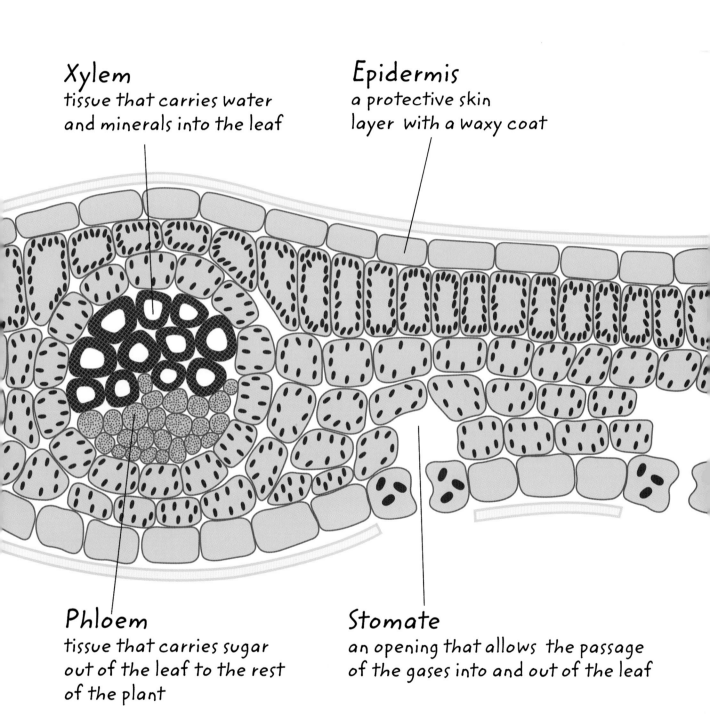

Xylem
tissue that carries water
and minerals into the leaf

Epidermis
a protective skin
layer with a waxy coat

Phloem
tissue that carries sugar
out of the leaf to the rest
of the plant

Stomate
an opening that allows the passage
of the gases into and out of the leaf

Plants Make Food—
Plants Are Food

Plants make their own fuel, and they are food for people and other animals. Animals that eat only plants are called herbivores. Can you think of some examples? Many herbivores, like cows, sheep, goats, and horses, eat grass. What part of the grass plant do they eat? Do you eat grass too? Actually, you do! When you eat cereal, you eat grass! But you eat a different part of the grass plant than grazing herbivores eat.

Supermarket Detective

On your next trip to the supermarket, take along a pencil and a pad of paper. Visit the breakfast cereal aisle.

Find the ingredients list on the side of each box of your favorite cereals. What is the first ingredient listed? Usually, the first ingredient gives you the name of the grass that was used to make the cereal. For example, you may see "puffed rice," "oat flour," or "milled corn." Write down each of these grasses.

What part of a grass plant is used to make cereal? The seed! Grass seeds are often called grains. Which grasses are used most often to make cereals? Rice, oats, corn, and wheat.

Popcorn
Grass Garden

You will need:

- Shallow flowerpot or other flat container
- Soil
- Popcorn (plain, not microwave) or grass seed
- Pebbles or gravel and larger stones
- Construction paper

What to do:

1. Fill the pot with soil to about 3/4 inch from the top edge.

2. If you like, plant the popcorn in a pattern. Cut out shapes of construction paper and place them where you don't want grass to grow.

3. Scatter the seeds on the soil. Cover the seeds with about 1/4 inch of soil. Keep the soil loose.

4. Remove the paper. You can make a "pathway" with gravel and line it with larger stones or add a seashell to hold water and make a little "pond."

5. Water the newly planted seeds gently with a sprinkler-spout watering can or a mister. Place your dish garden in a sunny location. Check your garden every day and water as needed to keep the soil moist but not soaking wet.

6. What part of the popcorn plant do we eat?

Food Chains: Everything Eats Something

Living things need food to give them energy to live and materials with which they can build up their bodies and grow and develop. Your body has gotten bigger and changed in many ways since you were born. You got the materials you needed for growing from the foods you have eaten. Where does your food come from? The refrigerator in your home? The grocery store? The farmer's market? Your garden? A farm?

Who Eats Who?

People are animals, and animals eat plants and other animals. Remember the herbivores? They are animals that eat only plants. Animals that only eat other animals are called carnivores. Many animals eat both plants and other animals, and they are called omnivores. People are omnivores.

Scientists describe "who eats who" in a food chain. In a food chain, the living things above eat the living things below. Whenever you trace a food chain back to where it begins, you will find plants. That is because they are the producers—they make food from "scratch," from the air, water, minerals, and sunlight they collect. Consumers must eat their food in the form of a plant or an animal. Consumers cannot make their food from "scratch" as plants can.

People (omnivore) = CONSUMER

Cows/Sheep (herbivore) = CONSUMER

Plants = PRODUCER

Life in the ocean also relies on living things that are producers. Most of these are algae, microscopic organisms that contain chlorophyll and perform photosynthesis. (So they produce oxygen, too!)

Pizza in the Food Chain

Each food that you eat is either a plant, made from a plant, or can be traced through a food chain back to a plant. Why are plants the original food producers for all life on earth?

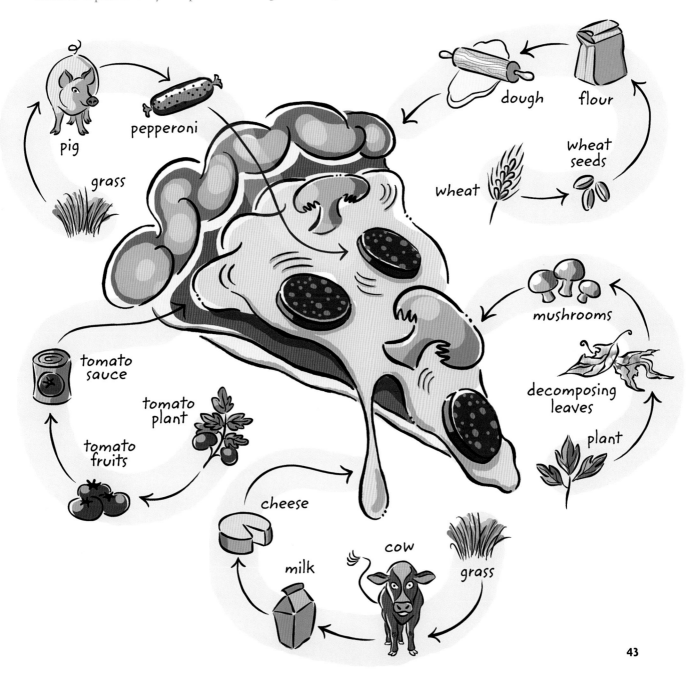

CHAPTER 3

Nature's Garden

Animals need plants! Roots, stems, leaves, flowers, fruits, and seeds provide food for all animals, including people. Plants are more than food, though. In the natural world, animals form relationships with plants that help them survive, thrive, and reproduce. Small animals use plants like trees, shrubs, vines, and grasses year-round to escape hungry predators and to take cover from heat, rain, and snow. Some animals use plant materials like leaves and twigs to build their nests each spring.

These relationships between animals and plants are not limited to the wild, though. They are found everywhere—in the trees on your street and elsewhere in your neighborhood, under your front porch or stoop, even in your houseplants. All we have to do is look and investigate what's happening in nature!

As gardeners, it's especially fun when we can find ways to garden the way nature does. Following nature's patterns requires careful observation of wild plant and animal communities and their habitats. It also requires understanding how plant growth relates to the soil, rainfall, and the seasons. By observing nature's ways, we can learn what plants and animals need and then create gardens that are beneficial for both—and provide fun and food for ourselves, too.

Look High, Look Low

Step outside into your garden, street, or park and take a good look around you. Everywhere you look, nature is busy: Plants are growing, flowering, making seeds. Animals are eating, building, hunting, scavenging. Take a few minutes to observe some of the animals' activities. What creatures do we share our community with, and what are they up to?

Scavenger Hunt

Visit a mature tree. Look for nests or leaf piles up high in the trees' branches. Can you spot holes in the tree trunk? What animal homes can you find?

Animals are constantly at work—searching for food and building their homes. Often they are doing both! What kinds of building materials do they use?

Animals are very creative in finding objects from their community to build homes with. Sometimes they include human-made stuff like paper, plastic, or fabric. Can you spot nest materials that aren't natural?

Go on a neighborhood scavenger hunt to gather some of nature's treasures. There are lots of things to collect if you look carefully!

Use this list as inspiration:

Acorn	Small rock	Fruit
Green leaf	Bark	Feather
Twigs	Nut	Grass

How many things did you find?

Animal Homes

You can create an animal home yourself using the materials you collected.

If you have lots of long, bendable pieces (grass, leaves, branches), try weaving them together to make a nest.

If you have lots of loose objects, find a small box to arrange them in. If you like, use pine sap, mud, or glue to hold your treasures in place in your box.

Imagine who might live in your nest, and how they would use it! While you are assembling your nest, pretend to be the animal living there.

The World in a Tree

It's easy to find a whole world of nature wrapped into the neat package of a tree! Why not "adopt" a tree of your very own to observe and care for? Watch how it grows and changes, and find out what you can do to help it!

Adopt a Tree

Try to find a tree in your neighborhood that is taller than 10 feet and has a thick trunk—it's likely to have more animals and other fun things to observe than a smaller tree.

Use a field guide to find the name of your tree. Get clues from the leaves and the tree's shape. If it's winter and there are no leaves, you'll have to be a tree detective and use other clues—leaf buds, branch shape, or bark texture. Once you know its name, you can do research to learn where it is from and find out how people and animals use it.

Adopting a tree also means caring for it as it grows. Remove litter from around your tree. Maybe you could plant shade-loving plants under it and mulch the soil to keep the roots cool. Water your tree if the leaves are wilting or the soil is very dry. Check for broken branches or marks on the trunk. (If it's on public land, parents may want to report damage to the local parks department.)

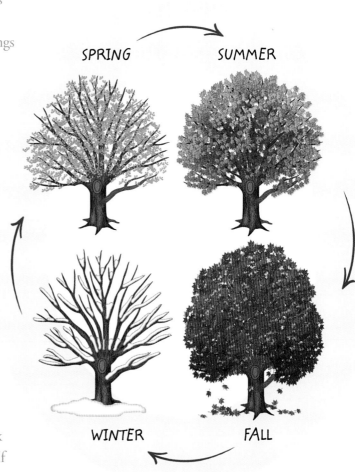

SPRING   SUMMER

WINTER   FALL

Trees help make life on earth possible. Taken together, trees capture almost half of the sun's energy photosynthesized by terrestrial organisms.

Tree Journal

At least once a month, visit your tree and record observations about your tree and how it is changing. You can use your nature journal or start a new notebook just for your tree.

RUBBINGS

To make leaf or bark rubbings, place paper over a leaf or a section of bark. Gently rub the side (not the point) of a pencil or crayon across the paper. Do you see the imprint of the leaf or bark coming through?

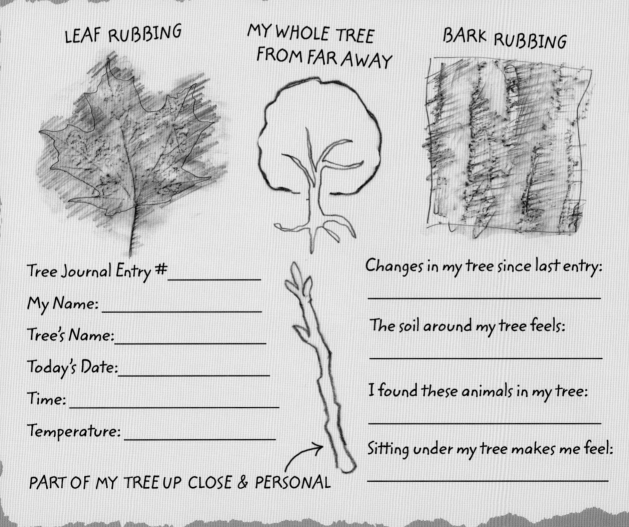

LEAF RUBBING

MY WHOLE TREE FROM FAR AWAY

BARK RUBBING

Tree Journal Entry #_____

My Name: _____

Tree's Name:_____

Today's Date:_____

Time: _____

Temperature: _____

PART OF MY TREE UP CLOSE & PERSONAL

Changes in my tree since last entry:
_____

The soil around my tree feels:
_____

I found these animals in my tree:
_____

Sitting under my tree makes me feel:
_____

Nature's Lunchbox

Look around your nature community at all the bustling activity going on. Animals are always on the move, but just what are they up to? They're looking for food, of course! All animals, including people, need food to grow and thrive.

Who Eats What?

We never see squirrels with acorns standing in line at the supermarket or birds purchasing seed from the hardware store, so where do they find the food they need to survive?

Look closely at the activity going on in your nature neighborhood. By following animals on their routes, you can gather clues about what they eat and how they find nourishment for themselves and their families.

Write or draw in your nature journal what you see outside. Write down or draw pictures of the animals you observe, what they like to eat, and where they find it! Try to draw pictures of the plant parts that are commonly eaten by wildlife. Can you identify any of the plants?

If you grow many different plants that produce seeds at different times of the year, animals can find something to snack on year-round.

Bird Feeder

You will need:

- 1- or 2-liter plastic bottle
- 2 sticks (like chopsticks)
- String for hanging feeder
- Scissors
- Birdseed

What to do:

Make feeding holes for the birds: Use the scissors to poke two dime-size holes on opposite sides of the bottle near the bottom. Poke two more holes into the bottle closer to the top.

Make two landing platforms: Turn your bottle upside down and make small holes underneath the feeding holes. Slide the stick through the small holes. Make two more small holes to run string through for hanging the feeder.

Purchase birdseed: Pick a bag with seeds in different shapes and sizes. Fill your feeder with seeds and hang it in a tree or another place that's at least 5 feet off the ground.

Use a bird identification guide to learn the names of the birds that visit your feeder. What types of seeds do they like? Seeds are a high-energy, nutritious food that many kinds of animals like to eat! Do any other animals visit your feeder from time to time?

BIRD BEAK SHAPES

Did you know? The shape of a bird's beak is a clue to its diet!

Insect-eating birds often have straight, narrow bills that work well for picking up tiny bugs.

Seed-eating birds generally have short, thick bills for cracking hard seed coats.

Making a Wildlife Garden

You've observed where animals search for food, what they eat, and how they build their homes. Are you ready to create a wildlife habitat to provide what animals need to survive and thrive?

Wildlife Garden Needs

Food

Garden plants provide nutritious food. Trees and shrubs make fruits and seeds that many animals like. Perennial plants and grasses provide flower nectar, tasty leaves, and seeds year after year. Annual flowers provide nectar, seeds, and leaves from spring to fall.

Gardening Tip: Animals need food year-round. If you choose a variety of plants that produce flowers and fruits at different times, animals will find food most of the year. In winter, when food sources are limited, set out bird feeders.

Shelter

Garden plants are perfect places for wildlife to perch, hide, or build a nest. Trees are good for climbing animals and many birds. Shrubs and vines are popular with ground-nesting animals and birds. Low grasses and leaf and brush piles serve as hiding places for small animals. Mulch, such as decaying leaves, shredded wood, bark, compost, or straw, is good shelter for small animals. (It also helps conserve soil moisture and keeps weeds away.) Fallen branches or trees make great habitat for lots of wildlife.

Gardening Tip: Combine different types of plants in a variety of shapes and sizes to allow many animal visitors to share a small space.

Native Plants

Many plants have grown wild in your region for thousands of years and probably much longer. They thrive in the local climate and soil. They are great at providing food and shelter for animal visitors who have been living with these plants for a long time.

Gardening Tip: Check in with your local nature center for a list of native plants that are especially beneficial for wildlife in your area.

Water

Water is necessary for both plants and animals to survive. Set out saucers, dishes, and trays of water in open spaces. Clean and refill them regularly year-round. See who comes by for a bath or a quick drink!

Gardening Tip: If you have time and space, create a small pond in your garden for water-loving plants, amphibians, and reptiles.

Human Visitors

Make a perch for yourself and friends where you can sit and observe your new habitat garden come to life around you!

A Model Wildlife Garden

On the previous page, you read about the ingredients for a wildlife garden. Now look at the garden on this page. Do you think animals would come to visit this garden? Do you think they would be able to live here?

55

Feeding People—Spring

When you make a wildlife garden you help take care of animals. How about people? What can you grow for us? Vegetables and fruits, of course! Remember the most important things that plants need to grow: light, soil, space, and water. A good place for a vegetable garden is flat and gets at least six hours of sunlight a day. If possible, choose a spot that is protected from wind and pollution and has some space for playing.

Spring Garden

You will need:

- Seeds of cool-season vegetables like beets, carrots, lettuce, peas, radishes, and spinach
- Compost
- Garden tools: trowel, spade, rake, hoe

What to do:

Sketch out your garden plan. Mark the edges of the garden with rocks or a small fence.

Mix compost into the soil, about 5 to 6 inches deep.

Sow seeds according to the directions on the seed packets. Thin the seedlings as they start to grow. Taste the ones that you thin. Do seedlings taste like the grown plants, or do they have their own flavor?

Use labels to mark the names of vegetables, the date planted, and the grower's name.

Add mulch between the plants to protect the soil, preserve water, and keep down weeds.

Harvest your vegetables when they are ready, and sow new seeds throughout spring to extend your harvest into early summer. Enjoy!

Knee-High Garden for Knee-High Gardeners

If you have little or no ground space for a garden, or if you would like to keep your plants grouped together off the ground, container gardening is the way to grow! If you choose lightweight materials, you can easily move your garden around.

You will need:

- 1 or more containers with drainage holes
- Pebbles
- Planting mix (potting soil combined with compost is good)
- Seeds of cool-season vegetables like beets, carrots, lettuce, peas, radishes, and spinach

What to do:

Place a layer of pebbles or gravel in the bottom of each container to help with drainage.

Fill the container nearly to the top with the planting mix. Moisten the mix by adding a little water if it feels dry.

Sow seeds. Follow the instructions on the seed packets. Thin the seedlings to be sure to leave plenty of space for your vegetables to grow.

Water the container when the soil feels dry. In a few weeks, you can start harvesting!

Feeding People—Summer

Summer is a terrific time to spend outdoors in your garden. You can plant warm-season crops, watch your plants flower and make fruits, and care for your garden—and then enjoy the harvest bounty!

Summer Garden

You will need:

- Seeds or seedlings of warm-season vegetables like beans, corn, cucumbers, eggplants,* gourds, peppers,* pumpkins, squash, tomatoes,* tomatillos,* and zucchini*
- Compost
- Garden tools: trowel, spade, rake, hoe

*You can start these plants in pots indoors in spring, then transplant them into the garden once the soil warms.

What to do:

Check local frost dates and recommended planting times to make sure the soil is warm enough for summer crops.

If you are starting a new garden, follow steps 1 and 2 on page 56. If you already have a garden, sow seeds or plant seedlings as your spring vegetables are finishing.

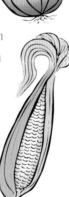

Spread mulch between your plants to keep weeds away and conserve water.

Water your vegetables when the soil feels dry. Apply a little organic fertilizer like fish or seaweed emulsion every two weeks.

Support tomato, tomatillo, and pepper plants with stakes if they start to lean over.

You can also grow herbs with your vegetables. Basil, chives, cilantro, lemon balm, mint, parsley, and sage are all tasty. Use seeds or buy potted seedlings.

How about some flowers with your vegetables? Sunflower, nasturtium, coreopsis, bee balm, calendula, and marigold are pretty and easy to grow from seed, and guess what—they taste good too!

Salsa Garden

This garden is perfect for a window box or a large pot. See instructions on page 57 to get your container started. You can also grow these plants in a sunny spot in your garden!

You will need:

- 1 plum tomato seedling
- 1 jalapeño chile pepper seedling
- 1 tomatillo seedling
- 3 garlic cloves
- 1 or 2 cilantro seedlings
- Pot, window box, or garden plot

What to do:

Plant the tomato, tomatillo, and chile pepper seedlings 6 inches apart. Add the cilantro plants at either end. Tuck the garlic cloves between the other plants, burying half the clove under the soil. Water your plants well.

Harvest Your Salsa!

You will need:

- 2 chopped tomatoes
- 2 husked and chopped tomatillos
- 1 peeled and chopped clove garlic
- 1 chopped and seeded jalapeño chile
- 2 tablespoons chopped cilantro
- Juice of 1 lime
- 1/4 teaspoon salt and a little pepper

What to do:

Combine all the ingredients in a small bowl. Stir your mixture well and refrigerate for one hour before serving. Enjoy!

Garden Hideaways

Earlier in this chapter you were looking for animal homes in your garden and neighborhood and perhaps making some nests from materials that you found. How about you? Would you like a little home in your garden? Find out how to use vines and sunflowers to make kid-size shelters. Move in and watch them grow!

Tepee Shelter

You will need:
- Seeds of fast-growing vines such as scarlet runner bean (they have edible red flowers that attract pollinators); hyacinth bean (the colorful flowers and neat fruits draw lots of critters); morning glories (pink, blue, or white flowers attract hummingbirds)
- Compost
- 5 to 7 bamboo poles about 6 feet long
- Heavy twine

What to do:
Bury the bamboo poles a foot deep in the ground at an angle, so that they lean in toward each other. Tie them together at the top with heavy twine to form a tepee shape.

Run some more twine or netting around the tepee midsection to support the vines as they climb.

Plant the seeds of one or more vines 3 inches apart on the outside of the poles. As the seedlings start to grow, thin some out if they seem crowded.

Watch the seedlings climb up the poles. (You may have to guide them.)

Sunflower House

You will need:
- Sunflower seeds
- Morning glory seeds
- Compost

What to do:
Measure out a garden plot that's about 4 feet by 8 feet. Work compost into the soil.

After the last frost, plant the sunflower seeds 1 foot apart around the edge of the plot, leaving 2 feet open for the "door." Plant the morning glory seeds next to the sunflower seeds.

As the morning glories grow, they will twine around the sunflower stems. When they are taller than the sunflowers, wrap them across the top to form a "roof." Ready to move in!

Sunflower seeds are tasty—if you can get them before the birds do! Harvest the seeds when the flower petals have fallen: Cut each flower head and hang it upside down by its stem in a dry, warm room. When the seeds are dry, rub your hands across the flower head so that the seeds fall out. Save the seeds to eat, to feed to the birds in winter, or to plant next year.

Fall and Winter in the Garden

Fall is a terrific time to watch your plants make fruits and seeds. Harvest the food bounty to savor now and preserve for later! Save seeds from the garden to plant next year. Make bird feeders and birdhouses. Then start putting your garden to bed for the cold days ahead.

Gourd Wren House

You will need:
- Round, pear-shaped, or oblong gourd harvested from your summer garden
- Lacquer and paint
- Sandpaper, string (or wire)

What to do:

Dry your gourd in a warm, dark place for four to five weeks or until you can hear the seeds rattle when you shake it.

Make a small hole, no larger than 1-1/2 inches in diameter. This is the entrance. Make some small holes in the bottom for drainage. Make two holes near the top for hanging the gourd with string or wire.

Lightly sand the gourd and apply a lacquer to harden and preserve it. Then paint it anyway you like. Next spring hang the wren house in a tree. Watch for visitors.

Preparing for Winter

Pull out spent vegetable plants and put them on the compost pile. Be careful with other plants, though—many are just resting until spring! Test them with the bending trick: If they bend easily, they're probably alive. If they snap and break, they're most likely dead. Or scratch a small piece of bark back from the stem—if there's green underneath, it's alive. Amend the soil around live plants with compost and mulch, like chopped leaves.

Snowy Critter Clues

You may see signs of animal activity in winter, when you would think the food was all gone. Animals are scavenging for fruits and seeds dropped in fall, and boy, are they hungry now! Can you spot animal tracks in the snow?

Treats for Birds

- Pinecones smeared with peanut butter or sunflower butter, then rolled in birdseed
- Small mesh bags of beef suet
- Nosegays of wheat and other grains
- Rinds of orange halves filled with birdseed
- Dried sunflower heads or small ears of corn

Treats for People

Drying is a fun way to preserve tomatoes, apples, and other fresh fruits. Slice your fruits crosswise into 1/2-inch slices. Bake them in the oven on baking sheets at 200°F. for two to three hours, or look at the library or online for instructions for drying them in the sun.

CHAPTER 4

Plants Need Animals!

**A**ll animals, including us, depend on plants to survive. But plants also depend on animals like birds, insects, and people for their survival! They often rely on animal help for two processes essential to their reproduction: pollination and seed dispersal.

Before a plant can begin to produce seeds, it must be pollinated. Flowering plants have evolved to produce flower shapes, colors, and nectars that attract pollinators to their reproductive parts. When a flower is pollinated, pollen grains (male gametes) are moved from a flower's anthers to the ovules (female gametes) through the stigma of the flower.

The pollen travels through the stigma and pollen tube to the ovules and fertilizes them. Then the ovary of the flower swells into a fruit that holds the developing seeds inside.

Once a flower is pollinated and begins to produce seeds, the parent plant needs to ensure that its seeds will land in some spot where they have enough sunlight, space, water, and nutrients to grow. This is where animals come in again. Some seeds are light enough to travel with the wind or in water, but many seeds travel with the help of animals. Some stick to an animal's fur and hitch a free ride. Others are collected by animals like squirrels that bury them and may not get around to digging them up and eating them.

People are seed movers too! For as long as people have been growing plants to eat, we have been collecting and planting the seeds, spreading them all over the world. Every time you plant a seed in your garden, you are doing your part to help plants reproduce.

Zooming in on Flowers

We all know flowers, but what are they made of, and why do plants have them? The flower contains all of the reproductive parts of the plant. The pollen is contained inside the anthers. It is usually yellow or orange and powdery. During pollination, the pollen moves from the anther to the stigma and down the pollen tube to the ovules. Pollination must occur before the ovules can develop into seeds.

Dissecting a Flower

You will need:

- A "perfect" flower, such as a lily, daffodil, tulip, or a flower from apple, garlic, onion, pepper, or tomato. (A perfect flower has both male and female parts. An imperfect flower, such as squash or melon, does not.)
- Card stock or construction paper
- Glue

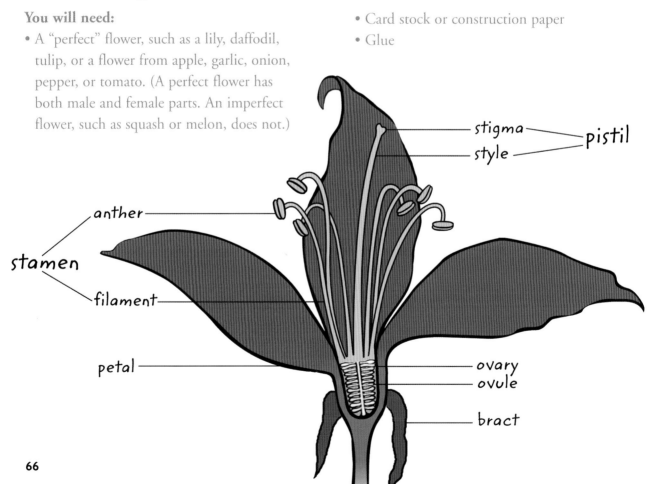

What to do:

Look at the top of the stem just below the flower. On most flowers, you will see parts that look a little like petals but are most likely green. These are **sepals**. (The flower on the left is an amaryllis, which doesn't have any.)

Now take a look at the **petals**. The petals protect the other parts inside the flower. Their shape, color, and arrangement are usually designed to attract pollinators.

Gently peel off the petals and look for the male parts of the flower—the **stamens**. They have two parts: the **filaments** are usually shaped like thin strands. Attached to their tops are the **anthers**. You'll find pollen inside the anthers. It is usually yellow or orange, but it may also be a different color. If you gently touch it, it will rub off on your finger. Try and see! If it doesn't come off, it isn't ripe yet.

Pull off the stamens and leave the thicker, central strand. This is the **pistil**—the female part. The tip of the pistil, which is often sticky, is called the **stigma**. During pollination it receives the pollen and directs it down the pollen tube to the **ovary**. The ovary is the thick area at the bottom of the flower, where the seeds form. Break open the ovary to find the **ovules** inside.

To make a model of a flower, arrange all the flower pieces that you have dissected on a piece of construction paper or card stock. Glue them to the paper. Label all the parts.

Now try this with other kinds of flowers you find. What parts do they have? Do they look different? Record in your nature journal what you find out.

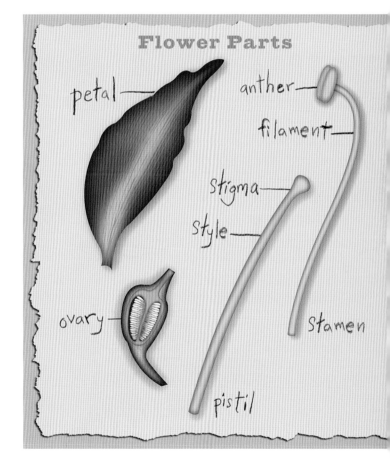

Flower Parts

petal — anther — filament — stigma — style — ovary — stamen — pistil

Sunflowers and dandelions are perfect flowers that belong to a special group called composites. A composite flower is actually made up of many tiny individual flowers that produce one seed each. Can you find the individual flowers on a dandelion? What about their parts?

67

Flowers and Their Pollinators

Most flowers are pollinated by insects and other animals called pollinators. Each flower is designed to attract just the right pollinators.

Pollination Partners

Flies are attracted to flowers that are brown or maroon. They love stinky flowers that smell like rotting meat or garbage.

Moths are drawn to light-colored flowers that open at dusk. Using their long tongues, they can drink nectar out of deep, narrow tubular flowers.

Hummingbirds love red, orange and magenta flowers that are loaded with supersweet nectar. They have long beaks to reach nectar in deep tubular flowers.

Bats prefer strong, fruity odors that they can easily find with their keen sense of smell. They love large, light-colored, night-blooming flowers brimming with nectar.

Butterflies visit red, orange, yellow, pink, and blue flowers. They need a flat surface to land upon, such as clusters of flowers or broad petals.

Bees go for yellow, blue, and purple flowers. They like petals with "nectar guides"—stripes that point them right to the sweet stuff. (We usually can't see these stripes.)

Plants produce bright flowers, strong smells, and nectar to lure pollinators to their flowers. The flowers are engineered so that bees, butterflies, moths, or hummingbirds brush against the pollen as they feed on the nectar; that way, they carry some pollen with them to the next flower they visit—and pollinate.

Pollinator Match

Read what kind of flowers flies, bees, butterflies, bats, moths, and hummingbirds like, and find the flowers in this picture that each one visits.

Super Flowers

You will need:
- Craft supplies, such as tissue paper, pipe cleaners, colored paper
- Markers, crayons, colored pencils
- Scissors
- Glue

What to do:
Design a flower with the different parts that you learned about on pages 66–67. Construct models of flowers that would attract bees, butterflies, flies, moths, hummingbirds, or bats.

Now make some pollinators and place them near the flowers that they love!

A Closer Look at Pollination

Flowers keep bees, butterflies, bats, moths, and hummingbirds busily pollinating. What about people? Can we pollinate a flower ourselves? Yes!

Pollinating by Hand

You will need:

- 1 flower bulb. Try growing amaryllis or paperwhite narcissus indoors in fall and winter. In spring, you can try pollinating daffodils or tulips growing outside.
- Pot and potting soil (for amaryllis or paperwhite narcissus)

What to do:

Plant the amaryllis or paperwhite narcissus bulb halfway into the soil in a pot just big enough to hold it. (Bulbs prefer to grow in tight spaces!) Water it thoroughly, but make sure to let it dry out a bit between waterings. Depending on the type of bulb, it should make beautiful flowers in four to eight weeks.

When the flower is in bloom, look for the pollen when it is released from the anthers of your bulb's flowers. The pollen is usually bright yellow to orange.

Look in the center of the flower and find the long white tube that has a star-shaped opening at the tip. This is the flower's stigma.

Use your finger, a paintbrush, or a cotton swab to move the pollen grains from the anthers of one flower onto the stigma of another flower. Do this until you have spread the pollen from each flower to all the other ones.

In the next few weeks, you will notice that the petals drop, and the base of the flower will begin to swell and grow. This swelling is caused by the ovules in the ovary of the flower developing into seeds. You are growing a fruit!

After about six to eight weeks, gently open the fruit to look for the seeds. What would happen if you planted the seeds?

Fruit and seeds of most bulbs are poisonous if eaten, so don't even think about tasting them!

Pollinating Your Vegetable Garden

Now that you've learned to hand-pollinate a flower bulb, you can try this pollinating technique in your summer vegetable garden. Almost all of the commonly grown fruits and vegetables are pollinated naturally by insects or wind or are self-pollinated, but we can help them along and ensure a bumper crop of produce by hand-pollinating in the garden as well.

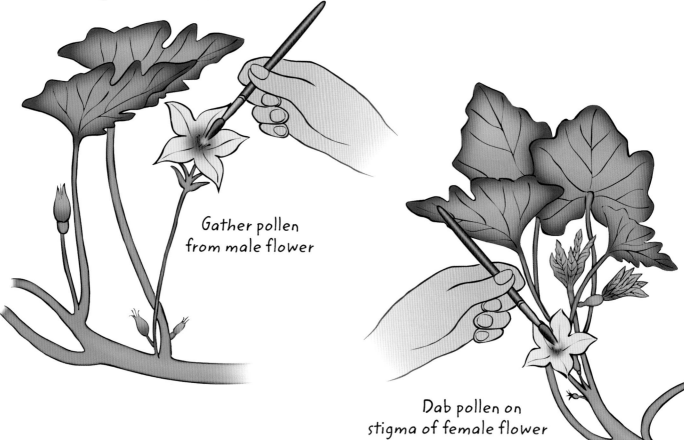

Gather pollen from male flower

Dab pollen on stigma of female flower

Hand-Pollinating Cucumbers, Squashes, Pumpkins, and Melons

These plants produce separate male and female flowers. They can really use our help, because the pollen has to travel farther to reach a stigma.

What to do:

1. Learn to tell male and female flowers apart: Male flowers usually appear first, grow off of side branches, and have a central stamen with pollen. Female flowers grow closer to the main stem, have a swollen ovary between the flower and the stem, and have a stigma in the center.

2. Find the male flowers and remove the pollen with your finger, a paintbrush, or a cotton swab, then dab it directly onto the stigma of a female flower.

3. Check on your plant every few days. In six to eight weeks, you'll be able to harvest the fruits of your labor!

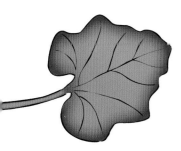

VANILLA ORCHIDS

The vanilla orchid produces vanilla beans as its fruit. The vanilla orchid is native to tropical Mexico and only has one species of natural pollinator, the melipona bee. This bee cannot survive outside Mexico, and no other insect can do its job. But people can! Today most of the world's vanilla is grown thousands of miles away from Mexico—in Madagascar—and it is hand-pollinated!

Pollinators in the Garden

Now we know that most plants need help from insects, birds, or bats for successful pollination. Without this assistance, fruit and seeds would not be formed. In fact, 80% of the world's species of food plants rely on pollinators for reproduction. It's time to go check out pollinators in action! They don't call them "busy bees" for nothing.

Looking for Pollinators

Find a spot near some flowers where you can sit for a little while and observe what creatures are coming for a visit (or a longer stay)! Make yourself comfortable so you can be as still as possible—you don't want to frighten away the pollinators.

Observe the kinds of plants you are near, what season it is, the time of day, and the weather. Come back to the same spot on other days, at different times of the day. Visit on a sunny day and on a rainy day.

Record your observations in your nature journal. Be sure to include drawings of flowers and pollinators. A model page is on the right.

Look over your journal page and see if you can answer these questions: Are different pollinators visiting at different times of day? How does the weather affect pollinators?

What colors are the flowers being visited? What shapes? Do the flowers visited by pollinators have any scent?

After observing which plants in your garden are best at attracting pollinators, you can design your very own pollinator-attracting garden based on your personal experience and observations.

Pollinators in My Garden

Date, Time, weather	Type of Pollinators Seen	Plants Being Visited	Pollinator Behavior
April 21 10:00 am sunny, warm	rubythroated hummingbird	red columbine	Hovering in the air, drinking nectar from the flower
May 29 3:30 pm some clouds, windy	honeybee	marigold	Buzzing around, landing in the middle of flowers and crawling around
June 18 8:00 pm just dark, cool	yucca moth	yucca	Fluttering around the flowers, picking up pollen from the anther
July 12 11:15 am sunny, warm	gulf fritillary	zinnia	Perched on the petals of the flower, fluttering its wings slowly
August 3 11:45 am sunny, hot	bumblebee	tomatoes	Shaking itself in the flower, getting pollen all over its body

75

A Garden for Butterflies

While you were looking for pollinators, you may have spotted some butterflies. If you provide warmth (a sunny spot), shelter (shrubs and trees), and nectar (masses of flowers from spring to fall), butterflies will start to use your garden to feed and maybe even breed. They also appreciate a small mud puddle in a sunny spot from which to drink water and take up salts and other nutrients. You don't need a big yard to make a butterfly habitat: A container or window box is a good start.

Butterfly Window Box

You will need:

- Window box that will fit on the outside of your windowsill (or another container)
- Potting soil (without pesticides!)
- Shallow bowl or jar lid
- Flat stones or small pieces of wood
- Annual flower seedlings, such as marigolds, dwarf zinnias, globe amaranth, and petunias

What to do:

1 Fill your window box with potting soil almost to the top.

2 Nestle a shallow bowl into the soil. Fill it with a thin layer of soil, then add water. Keep this "puddle" wet at all times. Butterflies will use it to drink water and gather nutrients from the soil. Refresh it every two days or so.

3 Transplant the flowers that you have chosen into your window box. Group several plants with the same type of flower together.

4 Arrange some flat stones or small pieces of wood in the soil around the flowers for the butterflies to bask upon.

5 Set your window box in a safe, secure place outside a window where you will be able to observe your new visitors.

6 Water your garden regularly—especially the first few weeks after planting and when there are dry spells.

7 Start a butterfly journal to identify the butterflies that visit. Draw or take photographs and try to find out the butterflies' names using a field guide. Observe and try to answer the following questions: Which flowers attract the most butterflies? Can you identify the butterflies? What time of day do you see the most butterflies? What different butterfly behaviors can you observe?

If you have a garden space to use, you can also make a larger butterfly habitat.

Feeding Hummingbirds

Hummingbirds are fascinating little birds that can make amazingly long migratory journeys every year. Some travel from as far north as Canada to as far south as Panama! They often fly 20 miles per day. During these long journeys, obtaining enough food from flower nectar is important. You can help them in their search for food by planting some of their favorite flowers! You can also set out a hummingbird feeder filled with homemade nectar to keep them coming. Ask your local nature center which months of the year hummingbirds can be found in your area.

Hummingbird Garden

The Best Spot

Ideally, pick a sunny spot for your hummingbird garden where you can easily observe the action. It doesn't have to be big. You can start your garden with three or four small plants. You can always add more plants later.

You can also plant a hummingbird garden in a window box or other container. (For instructions, see pages 76–77, steps 1 to 6.)

Water

Set out a shallow bowl and fill it with water. Like other birds, hummers enjoy a quick dip. Clean and refill the bowl every few days.

Nectar Plants

Hummingbirds are drawn to red and orange tubular flowers like bee balm, red salvias, columbine, and fuchsias.

Ask your local nature center to point out some favorite native flowers popular with the hummingbirds found in your region.

Plant three or more favorite hummingbird plants of the same type to provide a large amount of nectar in one spot.

For a larger garden, plant flowers that bloom at different times so that hummers can find nectar the entire time they are in your area.

To supplement the flower nectar, set out one or more feeders with homemade nectar.

HOMEMADE HUMMINGBIRD NECTAR

You will need:
1/4 cup sugar
1 cup water
1 or more small bottle- or saucer-style hummingbird feeders

What to do:
1. Place water in a small pan and heat it on the stove until the water boils.
2. Add sugar to the water. Stir it in and let it boil for one minute.
3. Remove the pan from the heat and let it cool.
4. When the nectar has cooled to room temperature, fill your clean hummingbird feeder. Store leftover nectar in a covered container in the refrigerator. (It will remain usable for several days.)
5. Hang your feeder in a shady area at least 6 feet off the ground. Choose a spot where you can easily observe the hummingbirds that come to feast. Clean and refill your feeder every two or three days.

Animals and Seed Dispersal

It's not enough for a plant to make seeds; it must also find a way to move them where they have enough space and water to grow. Some seeds, like those of jewelweed, shoot right off their parent plant. Some seeds are lightweight and can travel by wind. Other seeds travel by floating in water. However, many plants use animals to move their seeds around. Plants that use animals for seed dispersal usually do so in one of three ways.

Hitchhikers

Some plants have little dry fruits that stick to an animal's fur. The burrs you sometimes get on your clothes are not there just to annoy you. They are hitching a ride on you!

Super Poopers

Many plants that use animals as dispersers do so with yummy fruits that animals like to eat. But wait—if the animal eats the whole fruit, then it eats the seed, too. However, the seed is often not digested. Instead, it passes through the digestive system of the animal and comes out the other end. As a bonus, the seed gets dropped off with fertilizer! Some fruits have bigger seeds that animals do not swallow. The animal eats the fruit and leaves the seed behind somewhere.

Collectors

Some animals, like squirrels, have a habit of burying and storing nuts or other fruits. Inevitably, the animals do not retrieve all their buried fruits, and those left behind will have a chance to germinate.

fruit

burr

acorn

Seeds Dispersed by Wind and Water

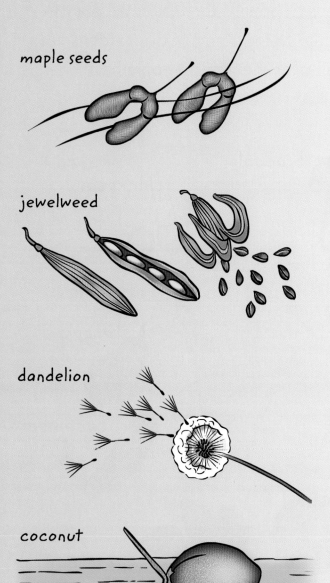

maple seeds

jewelweed

dandelion

coconut

Neighborhood Seed Hunt

You will need:
- Paper bag for seed collecting
- Construction paper or card stock
- Glue
- Pen

What to do:

1 Take a walk through a local park, garden, or just around the block. You'll be surprised how many seeds you can find! The best time to look for seeds outside is in summer or early fall—after most plants have finished flowering. Collect the seeds you find in a paper bag to take home.

2 Organize and separate your collection by size, shape, or color. How do you think each seed was able to move around? What are your clues? Use a field guide to identify the seeds you have. Glue them to the sheet of paper and label them. You've created a scientific seed collection!

Botanists around the world keep seed collections, called seed banks, that they use to grow new plants and share with other botanists in order to protect plants and ensure plant diversity.

Traveling With Plants

Take a look around your vegetable garden or a garden in your neighborhood. Most people grow a mix of different fruits, vegetables, and flowers. They may have started them from seeds or bought them as small plants. But where did they come from originally? Many plants in our gardens and on our dinner plates come from all over the world. People have been carrying around seeds of plants they liked for thousands of years!

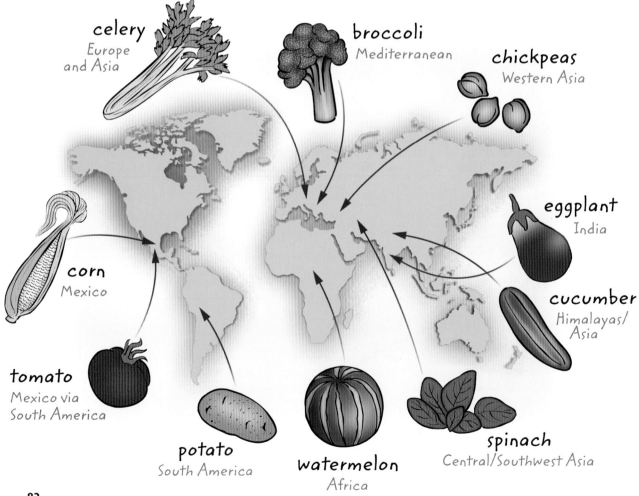

celery
Europe
and Asia

broccoli
Mediterranean

chickpeas
Western Asia

eggplant
India

corn
Mexico

cucumber
Himalayas/
Asia

tomato
Mexico via
South America

potato
South America

watermelon
Africa

spinach
Central/Southwest Asia

Seed Saving

Once you have started a garden, you will find that there are some plants that you especially like and want to grow again year after year. There's an easy way to keep these favorites in your garden: Simply harvest and save the seeds to plant again next year.

The best crops for seed saving are self-pollinated plants, such as beans, lettuce, peas, and tomatoes. They're most likely to grow true to type (which means the new baby plants will grow up to be like their parent plants). Not all plants make seeds for us to collect: Biennial crops such as parsley do not bear seed the first year. Hybrids do not come true from seed.

What to do:

Leave pod crops like beans on the vine until the pod dries. Harvest them before the seeds are dispersed. When collecting seeds from flowers, harvest the seed heads after they dry but before the seeds are dispersed. If the flowers have seeds that birds like, you may want to place a paper bag over the dried flower head to protect it. You can leave one flower head for the birds and keep one for yourself!

Once the seeds are dried, gently hand rub them to rid them of any chaff, then store them in an envelope in a cool, dry, rodent-free place.

Try to use your seeds within a year after harvesting. They will germinate better than older seeds.

CHAPTER 5

Nature Recycles

Have you ever forgotten to take out the garbage on pickup day? Does the unwanted stuff just disappear on its own? Think about what happens in nature. Where do all the leaves go that fall in autumn? What happens when plants die? What does nature do with all that dead matter?

Nature recycles! Special organisms called decomposers—insects, worms, bacteria, and fungi—break down dead plant and animal matter. When decomposers consume dead matter, they release the nutrients tied up in it, like carbon and nitrogen, back into the soil, the water, and the air. This is nature's way of replenishing resources. Gardeners take advantage of it when they make compost.

However, decomposition wouldn't work without one all-important ingredient: water. Water keeps every plant and animal in your nature neighborhood—including the decomposers—alive. Water allows the plants in your vegetable garden to grow taller, flower, and produce fruits and seeds. Gardeners work hard to conserve the water that all living organisms require to survive because, guess what: Water is another resource that nature recycles!

Decomposition in Action

What happens when you leave a piece of fruit like an apple or a tomato lying around for a long time? Does it change in any way? Maybe it gets soft and mushy or brown. There might even be some fuzzy stuff growing on it. That's nature's way of breaking down living—or organic—things right here in your house. Let's go outside and find evidence of nature breaking down dead plants, animals, and animal wastes into simpler matter that is rich in nutrients and ready for uptake by living plants and animals.

Decomposition Detective

Go on a hunt for the signs of decomposition all around you—in your neighborhood, in your garden, even in your kitchen!

Find a spot in your nature neighborhood that you would like to investigate.

What clues make you think that decomposition is going on? (Hint: Be sure to use your sense of smell.) Does the season have anything to do with what you'll find decomposing?

Draw a sketch of the area in your nature journal that shows where you found evidence of decomposition. Note the date. Come back to the same spot in another season. What changes do you notice?

Decomposition Corner

You will need:

- Pile of leaves
- Other plant matter like a twig, fruit, or seed
- Square of plywood or heavy cardboard (roughly 12 inches by 12 inches)
- 1-liter bottle of water
- Hand lens

What to do:

Find a quiet spot that already has a pile of leaves and add whatever plant matter you collected. Or make a small pile of your own.

Pour the water over the pile and place the plywood or cardboard on top of it. Leave it there for a week.

Check under the plywood or cardboard. What's going on under there? What is happening to the leaves? Have any new creatures moved into the pile?

Decomposers

Decomposers are changing the leaf pile into nutrients for the soil. Have you seen any of these larger new residents in your leaf pile? Do you notice anything else in the pile? Are there any white fuzzy growths? That's a type of fungus. Fungi are also decomposers.

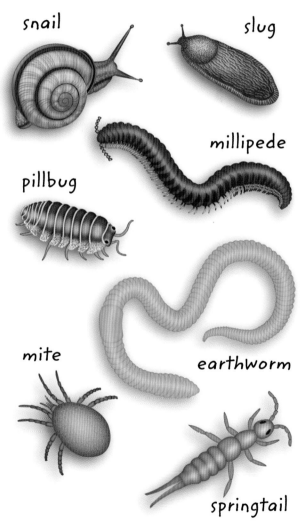

snail

slug

millipede

pillbug

mite

earthworm

springtail

Fun With Fungi

Fungi start as tiny spores that can be found in the air, on the ground, and on you! Mushrooms are fungi. Mold is a type of fungus that helps break down plant matter, including things we eat, like grains, fruits, and vegetables.

Growing Mold

You will need:
- 4 small pieces of bread
- Small sealable bags
- Cotton swab
- Mister spray bottle with water

What to do:
Take the cotton swab and rub it through a dusty spot in the house (on the windowsill, under the bed, on top of the refrigerator) to pick up stray mold spores.

Rub the cotton swab over the pieces of bread. Spray water onto them with the mister to make them damp. Don't soak them. Place the bread in bags and seal them.

Place the bags in different places. Observe them over the next week and record the changes in your journal.

Does mold grow better in a cold or warm place? How can you stop mold from growing? What happens if you try growing mold on dry toast?

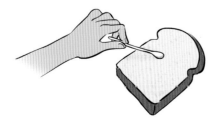

Mushroom Hunt

Mushrooms help break down dead plant and animal matter. Mushroom fruiting bodies (typically cap and stalk) must have just the right temperature and amount of rainfall to start expanding aboveground—and become easily visible to us.

Go on a mushroom hunt around your neighborhood. Set out after a heavy rain and take along a mushroom field guide. Fall, winter, and early spring are especially good times for mushroom hunts.

What mushroom shapes and sizes can you find in your neighborhood? Where do you find them growing? Do they have a scent?

Remember: Never touch or taste mushrooms that you find outdoors. Many types are poisonous.

MUSHROOM ART

Buy a portobello, oyster, or button mushroom at the grocery store. Gently twist or cut off the stalk. Set the cap, with the gills down, on a sheet of white paper. Let the cap sit for a day or so, and wait for the spores to fall out and leave a print on the paper.

Compost Science

Now that you have seen how decomposition works in nature, you can explore how gardeners use the power of decomposition to help their plants grow. Gardeners recycle vegetable scraps, weeds, and plant trimmings in a compost pile or bin to make humus, the rich top layer of garden soil that helps hold onto water and provides nutrients for the plants. Let's find out how to make this black gold!

Compost Ingredients

Every compost system needs a mixture of four main ingredients: green plant matter, brown plant matter, air, and water.

Brown matter (rich in carbon): Dried plant material such as chopped woody branches, fallen leaves, straw, cornstalks, sawdust, shredded newspaper

Green matter (rich in nitrogen): Fresh plant material such as lawn clippings and young weeds, fruit and vegetable scraps, tea bags, coffee grounds and filters

Air: The decomposers that break down your compost need air. Mix the compost regularly to allow air in.

Water: The decomposers that break down your compost need water. Your compost should feel like a wrung out sponge. Check it every few days and give it some water if it feels too dry.

Compost Experiment

You will need:

- 1 quart-size plastic freezer bag
- 1 cup greens (choose from the materials on the left) chopped or torn into small pieces
- 2 cups browns (choose from the materials on the left) chopped or torn into small pieces
- 1 tablespoon soil
- Spray mister bottle with water

What to do:

1. Put the green and brown matter and soil into the bag and mist it with water until the browns are moist but not soggy.

2. Seal the bag tightly with a zip top or twist tie.

3. Massage the bag daily to mix up the ingredients.

4. Open the bag every other day for six hours to aerate it. Then reseal it.

5. In your journal, make note of changes to the materials as they decompose. In two to eight weeks, you will have dark brown compost. What does it smell like?

December 15

Compost that smells bad usually has an improper balance of the four ingredients. Too much water, too little air, or too much green matter are the most common problems.

Compost in the Garden

You can start a simple compost pile in your yard: Recycle brown and green waste from your yard and fruit and vegetable scraps from your kitchen into a nutritious natural fertilizer for the plants growing in your garden or window box, the trees in your street, and your houseplants too.

Making Compost

You will need:
- 1 part green matter (see page 90)
- 2 parts brown matter (see page 90)
- Garden hoe
- Pitchfork
- Watering can or hose

What to do:

Find a quiet spot in your yard that's level. It should be at least 3 feet by 3 feet. Mix one part green matter with two parts brown.

Cover the pile with an inch of soil and mix it in well. Level the top of the pile.

Turn the pile every week to let air in. Keep the pile moist like a wrung-out sponge. You will have finished compost in six weeks to one year. It depends on how often you turn your pile and how well you keep it moist.

Use the finished compost in your garden: Either start your planting season by applying several inches of compost to your beds before planting, or apply compost around plants during the growing season as a mulch.

Use the compost for your houseplants: Sprinkle a little finished compost on top of the soil around each plant.

Compost Tea

You can use finished compost to make compost tea—a rich natural fertilizer for house or garden plants that gives them a boost of nutrients. Compost tea is prepared in a very similar way to the tea that you drink. You just don't have to boil the water!

You will need:
- Finished compost
- An old sock or stocking
- Bucket or watering can
- Water

What to do:

1. Fill the bucket or watering can with water. If you have chlorinated water, let it sit for at least one hour.

2. Fill the sock or stocking with compost and knot it at the top. Place it in the water.

3. Wait several days. When the water is a rich, dark brown, take the sock out and water plants as needed with the compost tea.

When fungi and bacteria break down plant material into humus, they also produce something else: heat. You can monitor the heat inside your compost and around it with a simple thermometer.

Soil Matters

So far in this chapter we have looked at soil as the place where most decomposition takes place and where decomposers live. But not everything in the soil is living organic matter. The largest portion of the soil is actually nonliving, or inorganic, matter. Let's take a closer look at the inorganic portion of the soil.

Soil Particles

The smallest nonliving things in your soil are sand, silt, and clay. Let's take a look through a magnifying glass!

Sand grains are the largest and heaviest particles. In a handful of sand there are large spaces between the particles.

Silt particles are much smaller than sand grains. There are also much smaller spaces between the particles.

Clay particles are the smallest and lightest particles. There are tiny spaces between particles, and they stick together easily.

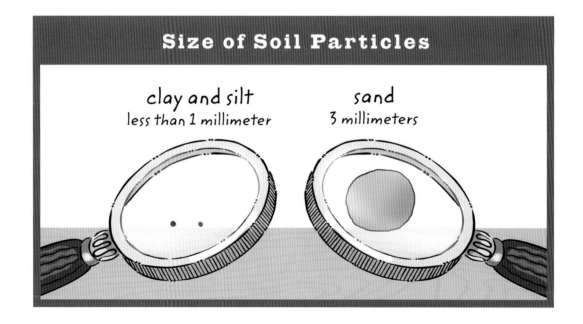

Size of Soil Particles

clay and silt
less than 1 millimeter

sand
3 millimeters

Soil Investigation

You will need:
- Plastic cup
- Paper plate
- Hand lens
- Glue

What to do:

Choose an area in your garden where you plan to grow plants, or choose a spot in your neighborhood where you want to find out more about the soil.

Scoop up one cup of the soil and pour it onto a paper plate. If you have a hand lens, use it to take a closer look at the soil particles.

Feel the soil. How would you describe the texture? Smell it. What does the smell remind you of? What colors do you see? What size are the soil particles?

Take another pinch of soil and put a few drops of water on it. Does that change any of its characteristics?

Note your observations in your nature journal and glue a pinch of the soil in your journal as well. (See the Soil Properties journal entry on page 97.)

Sand, Silt, and Clay

How much of each of the inorganic soil components—sand, silt, and clay—is in the soil varies greatly from place to place. How much of each is in your sample?

Mud Shake

You will need:
- 2-liter plastic bottle
- 2 cups of dry soil
- Funnel
- Water
- Ruler

What to do:

Fill the bottle with water until it is two thirds full.

Using the funnel, add soil to the bottle until it is almost full.

Screw the bottle cap on tightly and shake the bottle for one or two minutes, or until everything is well mixed.

Let the bottle stand for seven days, or until the water on top is fairly clear. Do not move it.

Measure the layers with your ruler. Use the samples in the journal page on the right to help you identify the sand, silt, and clay layers. Don't forget to look on the surface of the water. You might see plant parts floating there.

Soil Investigation

The soil feels (slick, gritty, sticky, other)
Slick and sticky

The soil smells (earthy, damp, dusty, other)
damp and earthy

The particle sizes are _tiny with a few medium-sized pieces_

When wet, the soil is _smooth and slippery._

Mud Shake

How many layers formed? _four_

What particles settled in each layer?

Layer 1: _Sand_

Layer 2: _Silt_

Layer 3: _water / clay_

Layer 4: _organic matter_

What else do you observe?
The water/clay is darker toward the bottom and lighter toward the top.

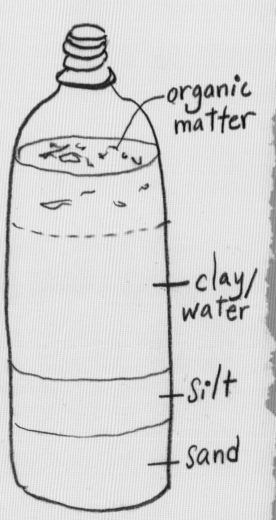

97

Plants and Soil

Together, the organic and inorganic matter of the soil can speed up or slow down plant growth. Try these experiments to see how seeds grow in different soil types.

Seeds in Different Soils

You will need:
- Packet of seeds (For quick results, use fast-growing seeds like radish or lettuce.)
- Egg carton with 12 cups
- Scissors
- Thumbtack
- Marker or crayon
- Mister bottle with water
- About 2 cups each of compost and sand
- Ruler

compost   compost/sand   sand

tomato April 27

What to do:

Cut off the top of the egg carton and use it as a tray. Poke a few small drainage holes in the bottom of each cup in the egg carton and place the carton cups on the tray.

Fill four cups of the egg carton with compost, four cups with a mixture of half compost and half sand, and four cups with sand.

Use the marker or crayon to label each section with the type of growing material.

Use your finger to poke a small hole in the center of the planting material in each cup. Place two or three seeds in each hole.

Place the egg carton in a warm, sunny spot and mist each cup with three squirts of water daily.

Observe your seeds over the next three or four weeks. Record your findings each week in your journal. How many seeds sprout in each soil type? How tall are the sprouts? What color are the sprouts in each soil type? How many leaves do they have?

Once you have finished your experiment and your seedlings have at least four leaves in addition to the two first leaves, move them to larger pots so they have room to grow. If you are doing the experiment sometime between spring and early fall, you can transplant the seedlings to an outdoor window box or to your vegetable garden.

Seeds and Soils

DATE				
SOIL TYPE	Week 1	Week 2	Week 3	Week 4
COMPOST				
Number of sprouted seeds				
Size				
Color				
Number of leaves				
COMPOST/SAND				
Number of...				

Nature's Water Cycle

All living things need water, but where does it all come from, and where does it all go?

Recycling Water

Take a look at the drawing. Follow the big arrows. Can you figure out how nature's water cycle works?

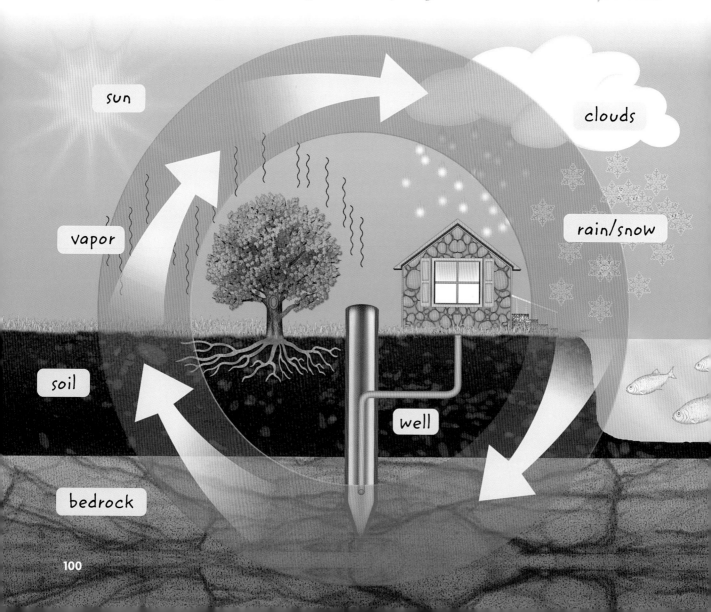

sun

clouds

vapor

rain/snow

soil

well

bedrock

Measuring Rainwater

When it rains, you can observe nature's water cycle in action. Do you know how much water falls on your garden or your neighborhood? Find out with a simple tool called a rain gauge.

You will need:
- 2-liter plastic bottle
- 1 or 2 handfuls of pebbles or small stones
- Utility knife
- Ruler
- Permanent marker

What to do:

1. Cut off the narrow top of the bottle and place small pebbles or stones in the bottom of the bottle to keep it from tipping over. Turn the bottle top upside down and insert it into the bottle.

2. Stand the ruler next to your bottle. Use the marker to mark measurements 1/4 inch apart on the side of the bottle. Mark 0 at the top of the layer of pebbles. Then add numbers to the marks.

3. Next time it starts to rain, fill your bottle with just enough water to cover the pebbles. Then place your rain gauge in an open spot to measure how much rain falls on your garden. Note the amount of rain in your nature journal. If you like, track the amount of rain from spring to fall.

5 ——
    —3/4
1/2 ——
    —1/4
4 ——
    —3/4
1/2 ——
    —1/4
3 ——
    —3/4
1/2 ——
    —1/4
2 ——
    —3/4
1/2 ——
    —1/4
1 ——
    —3/4
1/2 ——
    —1/4
0 ——

Water Cycle in a Jar

All water is recycled in the natural world. No water is ever added to what we already have here on earth. What nature does on a grand scale, you can re-create at home—in a large clear jar with a lid.

Terrarium

A terrarium is a mini-ecosystem that provides the plants inside with the soil, air, and water they need to live and grow. The only thing from the outside is sunlight.

You will need:

- A clear glass or plastic container with a lid. It should be at least 12 inches high and have a mouth that's wide enough for you to put your hand inside comfortably.
- Sand or gravel
- Potting soil
- Charcoal chips (for aquarium or plants)
- Piece of nylon mesh fabric, or fine-mesh metal screen
- Small houseplants such as African violets, begonias, ferns, Irish moss, spider plants, Swedish ivy, and oxalis
- Mister bottle with water

What to do:

Wash and dry your container. Spread a 1-inch layer of sand or fine gravel across the bottom. This layer provides drainage for your terrarium and keeps water from standing in the soil.

On top of the sand or gravel, place a thin layer of charcoal chips. This helps absorb odors.

Place the piece of nylon fabric or metal screen over the charcoal chips. Trim the edges so that the material does not touch the sides of your terrarium. The screen keeps the soil from sifting into the lower layers.

Spread the potting soil in your terrarium so that it comes up to about one third of the jar's height. It should be at least 2 inches deep.

Now comes the fun part. Choose a few small plants from the list on the left. Decide how you want to arrange them in your container, and then plant them so their roots are completely covered with soil. If you want, you can also add some small stones, moss, pieces of wood, or other decoration. When you are finished arranging your terrarium, add water so that the soil is damp but not soaked. Then put the lid on the terrarium and place it in a spot that gets some sun, but keep it out of direct sunlight.

Check your terrarium every day. You may need to open the lid from time to time to add more water or reduce the humidity inside. Cut the plants back as they grow and remove dead leaves. How do you think your terrarium is like the earth's water cycle?

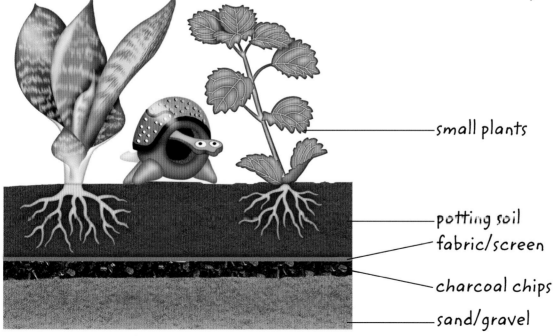

small plants

potting soil

fabric/screen

charcoal chips

sand/gravel

Nature Has More to Show You

ave you tried some, or many, of the activities in this book? Then you already know quite a bit about the natural world we are part of.

Did you explore how all living organisms depend on plants for their survival? Maybe you walked around your neighborhood and investigated how the animals in it get their water, food, and shelter. Did you make a garden to grow food for you and your family—and for animals too? Maybe you have seen the pollinators that help plants make seeds. Or maybe you have observed decomposers at work and thought about how nature recycles all its precious resources.

Good work! But wait, you are not finished. Your exploration of the natural world has just begun. Go back outside, keep your eyes and ears open, and keep investigating!

Glossary of Plant and Gardening Terms

Annual plants live for a year or less. In that time they grow from seeds into adult plants, produce flowers, and make and disperse seeds. Then they die.

Anther is the part at the top of the stamen of a flower containing pollen. When the anthers mature, the pollen is released.

Biennial plants live for two years. In the first year, the seeds grow into plants but do not flower. They rest over a dry season or over the winter. In the second year, they produce flowers, and make and disperse seeds. Then they die.

Botanic Gardens display collections of plants that have been chosen for their scientific, educational, and horticultural value.

Botanists observe and investigate how plants grow, how they function, how their parts are constructed, how they reproduce, and how they are related to one another.

Botany is the scientific study of plants.

Buds are usually found on plant stems, often just above where the leaves attach or at the tips of the stems. Buds can develop into new stems, leaves, or flowers.

Carbon is one of the chemicals that plants use to make sugar.

Chlorophyll is a green pigment—a colored chemical—that plants use to trap sunlight energy in the process of photosynthesis.

Communities of living things are made up of many different types of plants and animals that share the same space.

Compost is created when microorganisms, worms, and insects break down parts of plants and turn them into humus—the living part of the soil.

Consumers are living organisms that eat other living organisms, including plants and animals.

Deciduous trees and shrubs drop all their leaves at the same time once a year. They do this when a dry and/or cold season starts. When moisture and warmth return, new leaves start to grow.

Decomposers are living things such as fungi and bacteria that break down the parts of dead plants and animals. These nutrients are then returned to the environment and reused by other living things.

Ecosystems are made up of all the living plants, animals, and microorganisms in an environment and all the nonliving things such as air, water, minerals, and light that they need to grow and survive.

Energy gives living things the power source that they need to grow and reproduce. Energy can exist in active forms such as heat or light. Energy can also be stored in a form from which it can later be released to fuel the activities of a living thing. Sugar is a form of stored energy.

Evergreen trees and shrubs keep their leaves in all seasons of the year.

Fertilization takes place in the ovary of a flower when parts of a pollen grain join together with parts of an ovule.

Filaments hold the anthers of a flower.

Flowers typically consist of sepals, petals, stamens, and pistils. They are the reproductive part of a plant.

Fruits develop from the ovary and other parts of the floral structure. They contain seeds, and often their role is to disperse the seeds away from the parent plant.

Fuel, as used here, is the source of energy and materials that's held in complex organic molecules, and which plants manufacture from simple inorganic carbon dioxide and water, using energy from sunlight.

Habitats are the places where living things find or build shelter and search for their food—the places where they live.

Herbaria (singular: herbarium) are collections of preserved plant parts that botanists keep. Plants or branches with leaves and flowers are mounted onto paper and labeled with the plant's name and the date and place where it was collected.

Herbivores are animals that use only plants as their source of food.

Inorganic usually describes substances found in the natural environment that do not contain carbon and hydrogen. Inorganic substances include water, minerals, and gases.

Leaves are plant parts whose job it is to use sunlight energy to make sugars for the plant. Through the leaves a plant also takes in and gives off gases through pores that can open and close. These are called stomates.

Mulch is a material that gardeners use to cover the top of the ground around their plants to help keep the soil moist and prevent weeds from growing.

Nectar is a sugary energy-rich liquid that pollinators seek when they visit flowers. While collecting nectar, pollinators also unintentionally pick up pollen on their bodies that they carry to the next flower they visit.

Nitrogen is a chemical that plant roots take in from the soil. Plants need nitrogen to make the proteins that build their cells and tissues.

Nutrients are substances living things need to build and fuel their bodies.

Omnivores, including people, are animals that use both plants and other animals as their source of food.

Organic is a word that describes any substance that contains carbon and hydrogen, two chemical elements found in the natural environment. Sugars and proteins are examples of organic compounds.

Perennial plants live for several years and often for many years. They have developed strategies to survive regular, seasonal changes in their environment such as cold or dry periods.

Ovary is the part of the flower where pollen fertilizes ovules and where seeds are formed.

Ovules are located inside the ovary of a flower. Ovules hold an egg cell and nutritive tissues. When fertilized the ovule develops into the seed.

Oxygen is a gas that plants, animals, and most other living things need to live. Oxygen is made by plants when they manufacture sugar in the process of photosynthesis.

Petals are the parts of flowers that are arranged and colored in particular ways to attract and guide pollinators.

Photosynthesis takes place in the green parts of every plant when the green pigment chlorophyll traps the energy of sunlight. Sunlight is used to combine carbon dioxide and water to create sugar, an energy-rich substance plants use to grow and reproduce.

Pistils are located in the center of a flower. Pollen gets stuck on top of the pistil and then travels down a tube to the ovary at the bottom of the pistil, where it takes part in the process of making seeds.

Pollen contains reproductive cells needed to make seeds. Pollen is released by the stamens of a flower and carried by wind, water, or animal pollinators to flowers of the same species.

Pollination takes place when a plant's pollen is delivered (by wind, water, or an animal pollinator) to the stigma of a pistil of a flower of the same species. Pollen is needed to make seeds.

Pollinators are insects, birds, and mammals that collect pollen from one flower and unintentionally carry it to other flowers where it is used in the process of making seeds.

Producers are living things that collect energy and use it to combine water, gases, and minerals to make energy-rich substances such as sugars. Plants are producers.

Recycling happens when materials that were used for one purpose are recovered so that they can be used again.

Roots are the parts of a plant that hold it in the place where it grows. They also take in water and minerals from the soil around them.

Scavengers are animals that eat food left behind by other animals.

Seeds contain the embryo of a new plant and food and water that will be used by the embryo as it begins to grow.

Seedlings are young plants that have just begun to grow above the top of the soil after germinating from seeds.

Sepals are parts of a flower that enclose and protect petals and other flower parts before the flower opens. Sepals are usually green.

Stamens are the parts of a flower that contain pollen.

Stems support a plant's leaves and expose them to sunlight and air. Stems also carry water and minerals upward from the roots to the leaves. They also support flowers and fruits so that pollinators and dispersers can find them.

Stigma is the place at the top of the flower pistil where pollen needs to land so that pollination can take place.

Styles are the tubes that connect the stigmas at the tops of pistils to the ovaries at their bottom. The reproductive cells of the pollen grains travel down the styles to reach the ovules in the ovary.

Sugar is made by plants in the process of photosynthesis. Sugar is used by plants and the animals that eat them as a source of energy to live and grow.

Terrariums are (usually small) enclosed environments that re-create the right growing conditions for plants. Inside, moisture evaporates, condenses on the sides and top, and eventually falls back onto the plants and soil.

Weeds are plants growing in a garden that were not chosen by the gardener and that compete for water, space, and sunlight with the plants that the gardener does want to grow.

Taking Our Children Outside

Brooklyn Botanic Garden's first handbook for gardeners dedicated to the topic of gardening with children not only teaches children how to grow common garden plants from seed but encourages them to discover nature's cycles and follow their inborn curiosity as they explore many garden-related activities. It is our hope that adult readers will engage in these activities together with children, whether they live in your own household or in your community. Gardeners of all ages learn valuable lessons through raising plants; sharing this experience with a child is guaranteed to add an element of wonder and joy to your own time in the garden!

Plants are as critical to our very existence as air and water. Without them, we would have no food to eat, no oxygen to breathe, and very little rainfall over vast areas of now verdant land. What would our world look like without materials for buildings, fabric, or paper, or the vast array of medicines old, new, and as yet undiscovered that come from plants? Surely, without plants our planet would be simply uninhabitable by the human species.

Yet a majority of people in our society—children and adults alike—suffer from a condition that has recently been described as "plant blindness." We may appreciate a large, shady tree on a hot day, or the bouquet of flowers presented by a loved one. But for too many, the plants in the world around us rarely enter our consciousness. They recede into the background like an old, familiar pattern of wallpaper.

Of course, it's not necessary to think about photosynthesis with each breath in order to derive benefit from the oxygen in the air, but there is a danger in losing our collective awareness of the crucial role plants play in our lives. Our children can't be expected to be good future stewards of plants in the natural world if they aren't aware of their true value.

A preponderance of research in the last two decades clearly indicates that direct, frequent experience with the natural world produces positive physical, mental, and emotional benefits in children and adults. Improved cognitive functioning includes enhanced ability to focus, observational skills, recall of information, creativity, and the ability to reason. Reduced stress and increased self-esteem are also among the positive results when children are allowed unstructured time to explore the outdoors. Indeed, a growing number of specialists in child development now believe that regular contact with the natural world is essential to the emotional health of children.

Today in our society, children spend less than half the amount of time playing outdoors that their parents did at the same age, and much of that time is restricted to built playgrounds and highly organized activities or sports. Many experts believe that the unending complexity of nature stimulates positive development in children—something that can't be reproduced in playground structures designed by humans. Demographic analysis indicates that a rapidly growing number of children no longer have regular opportunities for playtime in nature. With more than 80% of the U.S. population now living in suburban or urban areas, we're raising a whole generation that's far removed from the natural world and the processes that sustain us.

Children from all academic and economic levels of our society have lost any concept that even the food we eat is directly connected to the natural world. This vital resource, around which so much of our culture revolves, has become disassociated from the natural and agricultural systems that produce it. To many children, food comes from the grocery store and is just "always there." In all but the most rural settings, there are few common life experiences that help children recognize that their latest meal came from the land, whether directly or indirectly.

What better way to connect children with the natural world than through gardening? The experience of gardening—planting a seed; watching it grow; nurturing the plant by watering, weeding, and guarding against pests; and waiting for it to bear fruit—teaches children many valuable lessons they will carry with them throughout their adult lives. Kids are much more adventurous in eating fresh produce when it comes from their own garden, and healthier nutritional habits, once formed, can last a

lifetime. Being responsible for the nurture of another living thing and creating something that is aesthetically pleasing develop personal values and connect a child with the larger human community and natural world.

Most of the formal research showing the benefits of gardening for children has been conducted in the past 25 years, but the findings are no surprise to us. For nearly 100 years, children residing in the largest urban center in the U.S. have been learning to grow flowers and food crops in the Children's Garden at Brooklyn Botanic Garden—the first such program in a public garden anywhere in the world. We witness, season after season, year after year, children move from timidity to self-confidence in the garden. We see them glow with pride when they take home produce from their own plots to be served on the family dinner table. We watch them develop strength and coordination as they learn to properly use and maintain garden tools. We quietly rejoice as we observe them developing skills in negotiation and problem solving while working collaboratively with their gardening partners.

Whether the children in your life have access to a large green yard or are confined to the growing space afforded by a windowsill planter, we urge you to share the joy of watching plants and the animals that live among them grow and flourish. We encourage you to participate in the gardening activities in this handbook with your child. You will find projects that can awaken the sense of wonder and nourish the self-confidence of children (and adults) in every setting. We can all appreciate the joy and amazement of discovering something new as we watch our garden and children mature!

—*Marilyn Smith and Sharon Myrie*

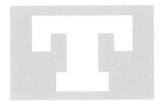his book is divided into five independent yet closely linked chapters, each of which explores an ecological concept. The first two pages of each chapter introduce you and your child to the subject matter; the following pages explore it with indoor and outdoor gardening activities, nature explorations, science experiments, and art and craft projects. How you and your child make your way through each chapter and the book itself is up to you. Take an ecological adventure tour and let the activities guide you through each chapter. Or browse and choose activities depending on what appeals to your child and you at any given time.

Be curious. Use the activities in this book as invitations to start gardening together with your child and discover the nature that's all around you. Enjoy the process, and be open for the surprises each of you may encounter.

Get dirty. Gardening activities and nature explorations require hands-on interactions with soil, plants, and water—some of which invariably end up on hands, clothing, and shoes. Make sure all gardeners and explorers wear comfortable clothes that are up to the task. And don't be afraid to get dirty!

Start a nature journal. A journal is a great gateway to investigating the natural world and keeping a record that can be referenced later. In addition to the journal pages suggested in this book, your child and you may want to record many other observations and activities.

Take time. Most activities are easily set up in under an hour. Spend as much or as little time with them as feels right to your child and you—you can always come back to the project later.

Use all your senses. Listen, smell, and watch with your child. Let your child experience the natural world with all her senses. Explain when it is okay to touch or taste and when to check with an adult first.

Handle with care. The activities in this book often require touching plants and interacting with living organisms. Model for your child how to handle living things with care and respect.

Be still. Observing nature may require sitting quietly for an extended period of time. This does not come easily to everyone. Work with your child, modeling the behavior and showing that being quiet offers its rewards and brings out the critters.

Garden anywhere anytime. A garden is a wonderful place to spend time with your child. If you don't have access to outdoor growing space, you can easily start a garden in a window box or on your windowsill. If the weather is less than inviting, pick an indoor activity. For inspiration, turn to the "Activity Guide" on the next two pages.

Grow a gardener. Introducing children to gardening is a wonderful opportunity to foster lifelong interest in nature and gardening. Take the opportunity to share the experience with your child. Overcome the setbacks that gardening invariably has in store and treasure the many enjoyable moments.

Activity Guide

Investigating Plants and Wildlife Online

Arizona-Sonora Desert Museum: Especially for Kids
www.desertmuseum.org/kids/

Bats
Bat Conservation International
www.batcon.org

Birds
Cornell Lab of Ornithology
www.birds.cornell.edu

Bird and Other Animal Sounds and Video Clips
Cornell Lab of Ornithology
www.animalbehaviorarchive.org

Butterflies
Children's Butterfly Site
University of Montana
bsi.montana.edu/web/kidsbutterfly

Discovery School: The Dirt on Soil
Discovery Channel
school.discovery.com/schooladventures/soil

Gardening With Children
Printer-friendly versions of the journal pages in this
handbook
www.bbg.org/gardeningwithchildren

The Great Plant Escape
University of Illinois Extension site for students and
educators that explores plant science
www.urbanext.uiuc.edu/gpe

Journey North
An educational website that engages children in the
study of wildlife migration worldwide.
www.learner.org/jnorth

Kids Domain: Recycling Links
Composting and recycling ideas for children
Kaboose
www.kidsdomain.com/kids/links/Recycling.html

Michigan 4-H Children's Garden
Michigan State University's interactive 4-H website
4hgarden.msu.edu/main

Microbe Zoo
Michigan State University
commtechlab.msu.edu/sites/dlc-me/zoo

Planet Plant
Botanic Gardens Conservation International's site for
children
www.planetplant.org

Underground Adventure
The Field Museum's site for inquiry-based science
explorations of soil
www.fieldmuseum.org/undergroundadventure

U.S. Fish and Wildlife Service Bird Pamphlets
www.fws.gov/migratorybirds/pamphlet/pamphlets.html

Worm World
Discovery Kids
yucky.kids.discovery.com

Online Gardening Resources

Brooklyn Botanic Garden
For gardening information on a wide range of
subjects, browse www.bbg.org/gar2

For a listing of composting resources visit
www.bbg.org/easycompost

International Seed Saving Institute
Tips for saving seeds of 27 vegetables
www.seedsave.org

Lady Bird Johnson Wildflower Center
Database of native wildflowers searchable by region
and growing conditions; links to native plant societies
www.wildflower.org

National Gardening Association
Introduction to gardening for children, with practical
tips for caregivers
kidsgardening.org

National Wildlife Federation Wildlife Habitats
Tips for starting a wildlife garden
www.nwf.org/backyard/food.cfm

Journal References

*Keeping a Nature Journal: Discover a Whole New Way
of Seeing Around You*
By Clare Walker Leslie and Charles E. Roth
Storey Books, 2003

A Trail Through Leaves: The Journal as a Path to Place
By Hannah Hinchman
Diane Publishing Company, 2001

Field Guides

Kaufman Field Guide to Insects of North America
By Kenn Kaufman and Eric Eaton
Houghton Mifflin, 2007

National Audubon Society Field Guide Series
Guides to North American birds; butterflies; insects and
spiders; mushrooms; trees; wildflowers
Alfred A. Knopf

National Audubon Society First Field Guide Series
Guides to birds; insects; trees; wildflowers; and more
Scholastic

Peterson First Guide Series
Guides to North American birds; butterflies and moths;
caterpillars; insects; trees; and more
Houghton Mifflin

Food and Wildlife Gardening Handbooks From BBG

The Best Apples to Buy and Grow, 2005, 2007
Bird Gardens, 1998
Buried Treasures: Tasty Tubers of the World, 2007
The Butterfly Gardener's Guide, 2003, 2007
Butterfly Gardens, 2007 (revised edition)
Designing an Herb Garden, 2004
Easy Compost, 2007 (revised edition)
Gourmet Herbs, 2001
Gourmet Vegetables, 2002
Hummingbird Gardens, 2000, 2007
Starting From Seed, 1998

To read excerpts of these and other titles, visit
www.bbg.org/gar2/handbooks.

To order books go to shop.bbg.org or call 718-623-7286.

Contributors

Monika Hannemann is the discovery programs coordinator at Brooklyn Botanic Garden. She oversees the Discovery Garden, an outdoor adventure garden for children and families. She also facilitates family drop-in programs in the garden to inspire young gardeners, scientists, and naturalists in Brooklyn and beyond.

Patricia Hulse is the children's garden and family programs manager at Brooklyn Botanic Garden. She has been exploring the wonders of science and nature with children and adults in urban, suburban, and rural environments since 1995.

Brian Johnson is an environmental education specialist with more than a decade of experience in the field. He has previously served as education officer for Botanic Gardens Conservation International, where he directed the organization's plant conservation education programs in the United States. He is currently pursuing a doctorate in environmental studies at Antioch University New England.

Barbara Kurland is the school programs manager at Brooklyn Botanic Garden. She has been teaching and learning about plants at BBG with children, youth, and adults since 1989.

Sharon Myrie, vice-president of Education at Brooklyn Botanic Garden, manages educational programs serving over 150,000 children, as well as adult education and community outreach programs through a wide range of initiatives. In 2003, she co-led the creation of Brooklyn's first environment-focused public high school.

Tracey Patterson has been teaching adults and children of all ages about plants and ecology in the garden, the classroom, and the community for many years. As an educator at Brooklyn Botanic Garden, she has taught hundreds of teachers and thousands of children about plants in the city and around the world. She is currently pursuing a master's degree in urban community health.

Marilyn Smith, director of children's education at Brooklyn Botanic Garden, has worked in the field of environmental education for nearly 20 years. She worked as a naturalist in Ohio and directed a nature center in Connecticut before coming to work for BBG.

SAm Tomasello illustrates nature, science, and fantasy for publishing, way finding, exhibits, and interactive media. Highlights of her career include illustrations for signage at the New York Botanical Garden's Everett Children's Adventure Garden, an exhibition of her extreme life-form images at the New York Hall of Science, and illustrations for McGraw-Hill Science textbooks. Her work was featured in the Guild of Natural Science Illustrators Exhibition 2005 and can be viewed at www.sciencepiction.com.

Sigrun Wolff Saphire, a senior editor in Brooklyn Botanic Garden's Publications Department, has been editing handbooks since 2000. She also works with schoolchildren as a volunteer Garden Guide.

Index

A

Animals
  homes for, 47
  plant foods for, 40, 50, 52
  seed dispersal by, 80
  tracks of, 63
  in wildlife garden, 52
Annual plants, 52
Anther, 64, 66, 67

B

Bark rubbings, 49
Bats, as pollinators, 65, 68
Biennial plants, 83
Birds
  beaks of, 51
  feeders for, 51, 78–79
  house for, 62
  as pollinators, 65, 68, 75
  and scarecrows, 21
  treats for, 63
  in wildlife garden, 52

Botany/botanists, 26, 32, 71, 81
Butterflies, as pollinators, 68, 75
Butterfly garden, 76–77

C

Carbon, 84, 90
Carbon dioxide, 25, 30
Chlorophyll, 30 31, 32, 38
Chloroplasts, 38
Communities, in nature, 4 5,
  12, 22
Companion plantings, 16–17
Compost, 56, 57, 58, 90–92
Compost tea, 93
Consumers, 42
Container gardens
  butterfly, 76–77
  popcorn grass, 41
  vegetable, 57
Cuticle, 38

D

Decomposition, in nature, 84,
  86–89
Design, garden, 22–23

E

Energy, 25, 30, 32
Epidermis, 39

F

Fertilizer, 58, 93
Filament, 66, 67
Flower
  in butterfly garden, 78
  growing from seed, 58
  parts of, 66–67
  perfect and imperfect, 66
  as plant part, 26, 27
  seed collecting from, 83
  sunflower house, 61
  See also Pollination
Food, plant, 40, 50
Food chain, 42–43
Fruit, 26, 27, 28, 71
  drying, 63
Fungi, 87–89

G

Gourd wren house, 62

H

Habitat, wildlife, 52–55
Herbarium, 12–13
Herbivores, 40, 42

PROVIDING EXPERT GARDENING ADVICE FOR OVER 60 YEARS

Join Brooklyn Botanic Garden as an annual Subscriber Member and receive our next three gardening handbooks delivered directly to you, plus *Plants & Gardens News*, *BBG Members News*, and reciprocal privileges at many botanic gardens across the country. Visit www.bbg.org/subscribe for details.

BROOKLYN BOTANIC GARDEN ALL-REGION GUIDES

World renowned for pioneering gardening information, Brooklyn Botanic Garden's award-winning guides provide practical advice in a compact format for gardeners in every region of North America. To order other fine titles, call 718-623-7286 or shop online at shop.bbg.org. For additional information about Brooklyn Botanic Garden, call 718-623-7200 or visit www.bbg.org.